D0398513

SON OF MAN

A PLAY

DENNIS POTTER

SON OF MAN

A PLAY

ANDRE DEUTSCH

FIRST PUBLISHED 1970 BY
ANDRE DEUTSCH LIMITED
105 GREAT RUSSELL STREET
LONDON WCI

MADE AND PRINTED IN GREAT BRITAIN BY
THE GARDEN CITY PRESS LIMITED
LETCHWORTH, HERTFORDSHIRE

233 96201 8

Son of Man originated as a television play. The television version was first shown as the BBC 1 Wednesday Play on April 16, 1969, with the following cast:

CHRIST:	Colin Blakely
PONTIUS PILATE:	Robert Hardy
CAIAPHAS:	Bernard Hepton
PETER:	Brian Blessed
JUDAS:	Edward Hardwicke
ROMAN COMMANDER:	Godfrey Quigley
PROCLA:	Patricia Lawrence
ANDREW:	Gawn Grainger

MAN IN CROWD: SECOND HECKLER:	} Raymond Witch
ZEALOT:	Brian Spink
ROMAN CENTURION:	Clive Graham
FIRST SOLDIER:	Godfrey James
SECOND SOLDIER:	Eric Mason
YOUNG OFFICER:	Robin Chadwick
FIRST PRIEST:	Keith Campbell
SECOND PRIEST:	Edmond Bennett
FIRST HECKLER	Hugh Futcher
MARK:	Colin Rix
LUKE:	Walter Hall
RUTH:	Wendy Allnut
WITNESS/MAN ON X:	Paul Prescott

WOMAN POSSESSED:	Polly Murch
BEATEN SAMARITAN:	Peter Beton

THIRD HECKLER:	Edmund Bailey
MONEY CHANGER:	Alan Lawrance
JEWISH GUARD:	Bryan Craven
BEGGAR:	David Cannon
BOXER:	Sonny Caldinez
BOXER:	Dinny Powell
THOMAS:	Michael Egan
MATTHEW:	Brian Croucher
JOHN:	Roderick Jones
FACTOTUM:	Harold Bennett
GUEST/CROWD:	Eileen Helsby
WOMAN/CROWD:	Maud Foster
WOMAN/CROWD:	Diana Payan
WOMAN/CROWD:	Greta Lewis
WOMAN/CROWD:	Svandis Jons
ROMAN LEVY:	Alan Tennock
ROMAN LEVY:	Martin Gordon
ROMAN SOLDIER:	John Biggerstaff
ROMAN SOLDIER:	Tony Rohr
MAN ON X/ TEMPLE GUARD:	Bill Straiton
MAN ON X/CROWD:	Whytam Greer

Directed by Gareth Davies

The stage version of *Son of Man* was first produced on October 22, 1969, at the Phoenix Theatre, Leicester, with the following cast:

JESUS:	Frank Finlay
PETER:	David Daker
ANDREW:	Stanley Lebor
JAMES:	Nicolas Chagrin
JOHN:	Graham Berown
PONTIUS PILATE:	Joseph O'Conor
COMMANDER:	David Henry
CAPTAIN:	Noel Collins
CENTURION:	Roy Boyd
SOLDIERS:	Paul Jaybee, Miles Greenwood, Michael Sadler, Noel Collins
BOXERS:	Paul Jaybee, Roy Boyd
CAIAPHAS:	Ian Mullins
JUDAS:	Stephen MacDonald
FIRST PRIEST:	Douglas Storm
SECOND PRIEST:	Stephen MacDonald
ZEALOT:	Andrew Neil
FIRST MONEYLENDER:	Douglas Storm
SECOND MONEYLENDER:	Roy Boyd
FIRST HECKLER:	Noel Collins
SECOND HECKLER:	Andrew Neil
LEPER:	Miles Greenwod
DOVE SELLER:	Andrew Jarvis
BRIGAND:	Andrew Neil
PROCLA:	Linda Polan
RUTH:	Liane Aukin
SERVING GIRL:	Penelope Nice

Directed by Robin Midgley

CHARACTERS

In order of appearance

JESUS

AGITATOR

ROMAN CAPTAIN

PONTIUS PILATE

ROMAN COMMANDER

CAIAPHAS

ANDREW

PETER

CENTURION

JAMES

JOHN

FIRST PRIEST

SECOND PRIEST

PROCLA

JUDAS ISCARIOT

RUTH

MONEY CHANGER

Roman soldiers, priests, hecklers, servants, leper, temple police, boxers, prisoners, money changer, men and women in crowd.

ACT ONE

SCENE 1

[*Darkness. Scattered shouts from the auditorium: 'He is coming!' 'He—is—coming!' 'Coming!' Howling wind. The lights go up to reveal the wilderness. A light picks out* JESUS *huddled into himself, high on a rock. The wind shifts up into a desolate whine. We feel that it is cold. The figure moves, but very little. He speaks in a dry-mouthed croak. He has been here forty days.*]

JESUS : Is it me? . . . is it—? Is it time? *Time?*

[*Silence. He huddles closer into himself. Then he lifts his head, like one listening.*]

Time. Time for—*I hear you.*

[*Pause.*]

I am listening. I am—oh, speak. Speak! Please, my father. Speak to me. Speak to *me-e*! My God. My God! God of Abraham and Mos— [*he gabbles.*] He is coming. It is time. It is time . . . time . . . time . . . time . . .

[*The word, repeated over and over, dies into him. He sinks down into himself, virtually comatose. Silence; then the light fades.*]

SCENE 2

[*A narrow square near the Temple in Jerusalem in Roman-occupied Judaea. Day. A wild Jewish* AGITATOR, *of the Zealot party, is haranguing a sympathetic but rather nervous* CROWD *of compatriots. As he rants a small troop of Roman soldiers take up positions on the fringes of the* CROWD, *virtually surrounding them.*]

AGITATOR: He is coming! He is coming! Have no fear! He will soon be here and in among us.
CROWD: He is coming!
AGITATOR: We are under the yoke. We are contaminated by unclean rulers and bullying heathens. But the God of Abraham and Moses and Joshua has not forsaken his children. The signs are in the heavens. *The Messiah is coming!*

[*The* CROWD *gives a low moan, half fear, half joy.*]

CROWD: He is coming!
AGITATOR: Yes! Yes! And the Prophets tell us . . . what do they tell us?
MAN IN CROWD: Clear a straight path!
AGITATOR: Yes! Yes!
VOICES: Prepare a way for the Lord!
AGITATOR: Yes! Yes!

[*The* CROWD starts *a moaning, rhythmic chant.*]

CROWD: He . . . is . . . com-ing . . . He . . . is . . . com-ing . . .

[*They press closer in to each other, and the* AGITATOR *whirls into a screaming fury of threats and oratory.*]

AGITATOR: The Romans have brought their blasphemous standards into the Holy City—banners of war which glory the divinity of their distant and unclean Emperor. It is a sign! God will come down upon them! The Kingdom of Heaven is upon us. The vengeance of our God is nigh!

[*The* CROWD *make a soft moaning noise and press closer into each other.*]

CROWD: Save us!

AGITATOR [*more frenzied*]: The Roman blasphemies are an insult to God and to the people of God.

CROWD: Deliver us!

AGITATOR: The Sadduccees of the Temple and Caiaphas the High Priest are hand in glove with the blasphemers and idolators! Until Pontius Pilate the Roman soldiers always covered their standards when in the holy city. But not now. Not now! They spit on us! They spit on our God! He sees. He sees! He will *not be* merciful—!

CROWD: Save us!

AGITATOR: Are we to swallow this dirt, like Caiaphas swallows this dirt? Are we to grovel before Pontius Pilate rather than kneel before the Lord our God? If we submit to the idolator what shall we do when the day of reckoning comes? For the day of reckoning *is* coming—is *now* upon us—now—!

CROWD: He is com-ing. He is com-ing.

[*The* ROMAN SOLDIERS *start to push their way into the crowd, very roughly.*]

AGITATOR: The sword will not pierce him. Flames will not burn him. Hypocrites and liars and belly-crawling traitors will not touch him, not one hair of his head . . .

CROWD: He is com-ing!

[*The* SOLDIERS *start pushing the people away, hitting and kicking them brutally.*]

AGITATOR: The idolators will be overthrown! The day of reckoning is coming! The Messiah will come down to his suffering people . . .

[*Screams as the* ROMANS *slash into the crowd with their short swords.*]

AGITATOR [*screaming*]: Clear a path for him, the King of the Jews! He is coming! He is com . . . !

[*The* CAPTAIN *of the troop claps his mailed hand over the* AGITATOR'*s mouth. The* CROWD *shout in fear.*]

CROWD: Leave him alone . . . leave him . . .

(*Two* ROMAN SOLDIERS *lift him kicking and struggling to carry him away. They are grinning.*]

FIRST SOLDIER: Wiry little devil, 'ent he?
CROWD: Leave him alone . . . leave him alone . . .
CAPTAIN [*shouts*]: Go home! Go home you stupid people or else you will be put to the sword! Get off the streets!

[*As he speaks, he draws his long sword. The* CROWD *subside into a sullen, barely held down silence. The* AGITATOR *is dragged roughly away through the crowd, one* SOLDIER *holding him by the hair.*]

CROWD [*murmurs*]: Deliver us!

[*The* AGITATOR, *kicking and struggling all the while, gains a momentary release. He screams out a defiance.*]

AGITATOR: He is coming! The Messiah is coming!

[*Harassed by the crowd, and flustered, the* CAPTAIN *plunges his sword into the* AGITATOR'*s stomach. The* CROWD *give a moan of pity and terror.*]

CAPTAIN: I told you! I told you!

[*On his knees, and gurgling blood, the* AGITATOR *lifts up his hands to God.*]

AGITATOR: The one who is coming is mightier than I am. Clear a path for him. Clear . . . ach!

[*One of the* SOLDIERS *has kicked him viciously.*]

SOLDIER: He'll end up where you're going, old friend!
CROWD [*hisses*]: He—is—coming. He—is—coming . . . The Messiah . . . The Messiah!

SCENE 3

[*The wilderness. As before.* JESUS *stirs, trying to get on to his knees.*]

JESUS: Is it—? TIME! Is it—me? *Me?*

[*He half pulls himself up. He begins to babble, almost demented by hunger, thirst and his sense of divinity.*]

Me? Me? Time has come. Me? It *is*—It is me, it is me, it is me, it is me—

[*He stops. He stands, swaying. Silence. Then he speaks, more slowly and clearly.*]

He went up into the wilderness. He went up—*I* went up and spoke to . . . Make straight the way. Clear a path. The Kingdom of Heaven is upon—ME?

[*Pause. Then he screams with the agony of the thought.*]

ME!? It—is—*me-e-e*!

[*Silence. He looks about him, as though for the first time.*]

Bread—oh, bread—br . . .

[*He stops, pierced by a thought—the first challenge.*]

If it *is* me . . .

[*He picks up a stone, almost falling as he does so, being so weak.*]

Bread . . . oh, to eat some bread . . .

[*He caresses the stone. He puts it up to his cheek.*]

He who is to come and fulfil the prophesies can surely turn stone into—into—

[*He bites on the stone. But, evading the challenge, he hurls it away in almost the same gesture.*]

Ach! The Devil speaks! *I shall not listen!*

[*Pause.*]

I tasted—bread—bread?

[*Pause.*]

It *is* me. It *is*. They are waiting and I must go to them . . .

[*He stumbles away, too weak to walk properly.*]

I must go to them. The Son of—the son of—

[*He falls.*]

—A—carpenter?

[*A shrill, harsh, almost demented laugh as the light fades on him and he begins to crawl.*]

SCENE 4

[*A street. A* LEPER *slowly passes, dragging himself along on a stick. His face and arms a scabby mess. His call is mechanical, matter-of-fact, mere routine.*]

LEPER: Unclean!— Unclean—Unclean—Unclean—

[*He stoops and picks up a scrap of something, pushing it hard into his mouth. He carries on the automatic cry, his mouth full.*]

Unclean. Unclean.

SCENE 5

[PONTIUS PILATE'*s residence at Caesarea, in Judaea.* PILATE, *the Roman Prefect, is addressing his senior military commanders. There is no doubt about his dominance, or his intellectual authority.*]

PILATE: I do not expect military commanders necessarily to accept the proposition that all Empires, past, present and yet to come, are based upon nothing more substantial than bluff. Mere bluff.

[*The senior* COMMANDER *makes a tiny gesture, almost concealed, of dissent.*]

Speak.

COMMANDER: Pardon me, my Lord—

PILATE: You may speak.

COMMANDER: I was only going to suggest, with respect, my Lord, that—well, that the soldiers—

PILATE [*raising hand*]: The soldiers lend *plausibility* to the bluff. Of course they do.

COMMANDER: Yes, my Lord.

PILATE: But when the battles are won and the territory is—pacified, then the civil power—here in this place expressed in the authority of myself, the Prefect of Judaea—has the far more difficult and perhaps unrewarding task of making citizens instead of corpses.

[*They laugh.*]

That is not meant to be a witticism.

[*Silence.*]

And the fact that you, the senior and therefore *presumably* the most intelligent officers should have considered my remark amusing only serves to emphasise what I have been saying.

[*Pause.*]

My orders have been and *are* quite explicit. They have not been obeyed in spirit, even though perhaps in letter. The soldiers are not to harass the people in their religious observances. They are not to approach the Temple in Jerusalem. They are not to exercise on the Jewish sabbath day. There is to be less deliberate provocation and less—

[*A* SERVANT *has entered.*]

SERVANT: My Lord!
PILATE: I am *speaking*!
SERVANT: My Lord—but it is the High Priest . . .

[*Pause.*]

PILATE [*to* OFFICERS]: *Dismiss!* Oh—Commander—I would like
you to stay.
COMMANDER: Sir.
PILATE: Perhaps it will help you to see.
COMMANDER: Sir?
PILATE: To see the point where the lance cannot penetrate. [*to*
SERVANT] Announce the High Priest.

[*The* SERVANT *bows out.* PILATE *seats himself.*]

All the soldiers on earth will not destroy what this Caiaphas
represents. Stay standing. And stay *silent*.

[*The* COMMANDER *tightens his face in disapproval as* CAIA-
PHAS *is announced.*]

SERVANT: Caiaphas, High Priest in Jerusalem, my Lord.

[PILATE *stands:* CAIAPHAS *stands still. They exchange glances
for a moment.*]

CAIAPHAS: I have come, Prefect, to request an audience of the
civil power.
PILATE: The audience is granted. We are pleased to see you here
in Caesarea, Caiaphas.

[CAIAPHAS *gives a tiny bow, little more than a nod, of acknow-
ledgment.* PILATE *sits. Only when* PILATE *is seated does*
CAIAPHAS *begin to speak.*]

17

CAIAPHAS: Pontius Pilate, my people are in distress.

[PILATE *looks at him, steadily.*]

PILATE: I am listening.

CAIAPHAS: Your soldiers have brought their standards into Jerusalem.

PILATE: Yes?

CAIAPHAS: Standards which have idolatrous emblems . . .

PILATE: Idolatrous?

[*Slight pause.*]

CAIAPHAS: To us. Yes.

PILATE: I do not understand.

CAIAPHAS [*angry*]: The Emperor is *not* divine.

PILATE: Are you denying his authority over this land and this people? [*Silence*] *Are you?*

CAIAPHAS: No.

PILATE: Well then . . .

CAIAPHAS [*quickly*]: But we deny his divinity and we will not deny the claims of God . . .

PILATE: *Your* God, Caiaphas.

CAIAPHAS: God.

PILATE: But Caiaphas, listen to me. The standards of the Roman soldiers have been carried to every corner of this earth. We are proud of them. They are our history, our blood, our bravery. And our mission.

CAIAPHAS: I understand that . . .

PILATE: Are you sure that you do? You prefer the claim of a God you cannot see and will not even name to the fact of conquest or the flesh and blood of the men who bear the standards.

CAIAPHAS: Jerusalem is a Holy City.

PILATE: We are not denying it. The Jews have been granted concession enough. And yet still the land is full of agitators and terrorists.

CAIAPHAS: There is tension in the air. The people are waiting.

PILATE: I know. I know. They await a new leader.

CAIAPHAS: Not in any way that you might understand, Pontius. It is not rebellion or insurrection that . . .

PILATE: Five terrorists were executed today. All of them died with the threat on their lips that there was one to follow who was greater than they. *Who* are they waiting for? What treason is being hatched? And is the Temple a—a centre for rebellion? We have not entered it or desecrated it or interfered in any way with it. What better place, then, Caiaphas, for raising the banner of wicked insurrection?

CAIAPHAS: No! No!

PILATE: You are the leader of your people, high priest.

CAIAPHAS: But not all my people accept that leadership.

PILATE: Oh?

CAIAPHAS: There is faith as well as blood in our veins, religion as well as marrow in our bones. Our God is also our leader, our protector. So when we submit to a superior earthly power, religious unity is difficult, religious dispute inevitable. Daily I too am abused by my own flock for working too well, too easily, with the conqueror.

[*Pause.*]

PILATE: I have given you many concessions.

CAIAPHAS: And I have not stirred up or countenanced rebellion.

PILATE: The standards are dear to our soldiers.

CAIAPHAS: Jerusalem is our holy place, never to be defiled.

[*Pause.* PILATE *is thinking, hard.*]

PILATE: If—I say *if*—if the military standards are hooded in some way within the wall of Jerusalem . . .

[*The* COMMANDER *stiffens with disapproval.*]

CAIAPHAS [*eagerly*]: Then a new era of co-operation and—
PILATE: Fewer terrorists?
CAIAPHAS: I think that—
PILATE: *Fewer terrorists?*
CAIAPHAS: You could count more readily on the co-operation of the Temple authorities in putting down zealotry and misguided fanaticism.
PILATE: You will *prove* that to me?

[*Pause.*]

CAIAPHAS: Yes. Gladly.

[PILATE *rises, a decisive gesture.*]

PILATE: The Roman standards will be covered when taken into Jerusalem.
COMMANDER [*protesting*]: My Lord—!
PILATE: Covered!

[*The* COMMANDER *bows.*]

You see, Caiaphas? It is not an easy concession for us to make.
CAIAPHAS: We accept it with proper gratitude and humility, my Lord.

SCENE 6

[*On the shore of the Sea of Galilee.* PETER *and* ANDREW, *brothers, are casting a net into the sea. Behind them, and unseen by them,* JESUS *approaches, stumbling down the hill from his fast in the wilderness.* JESUS *sees them, hesitates, and stops. He sits, watching them.*]

ANDREW: But everywhere they are saying it, Peter—

PETER: That still don't make it true, do it?

ANDREW: No, but—

PETER: The Messiah will only come when we don't expect him ... soon, maybe. Soon. I'll grant you that ...

ANDREW: You cried when you heard John. Out in the hills. Peter—you cried. I saw you.

PETER: Yah.

ANDREW: He said the Christ was coming. He said it. And I believed him.

PETER: Aye—but look at him now. Rotting in the dungeons.

ANDREW: That don't mean—

PETER: Ach—give it a rest! That's all we seem to talk about, all *everybody* seems to talk about—

[*Fractional pause.*]

ANDREW [*rather nervously*]: But—but if it *is* true—that's all there's *worth* talking about. Peter?

PETER: Shut up.

ANDREW: But Peter—

PETER: Oh, shut up! 'Course I want him to come. But how will he come? Like John—and end up behind bars? All right, he made me cry. Up there in the hills, he—

[*As he turns to indicate the hills, he sees* JESUS.]

ANDREW: What's up?

PETER: By God! Look at that, then.

[JESUS *gets up and walks towards them, still unsteady on his feet.*]

ANDREW: It's—ach, it's only a looney.
PETER: Watch out for your bread, then.
ANDREW: Perhaps he'll bring us luck.

[PETER *snorts. But* ANDREW *is staring with fascination.*]

ANDREW: Look—his feet are bleeding.
PETER: Take no notice. Take no notice.
ANDREW: Where's he come from, then?
PETER: We don't want to be bothered. Perhaps he's on the run.
ANDREW: He looks like—

[*He stops, a bit agitated.*]

PETER: Take no notice, Andrew. Keep yourself to yourself.
ANDREW [*hisses*]: He looks like—*John.*
PETER [*agitated*]: Shut up. Shut *up.*

[*As* JESUS *reaches them, they turn their backs pointedly. But* JESUS *just stands watching them, a little smile—almost of mockery— on his face.*]

ANDREW [*whispers*]: *He looks like John.*
PETER [*agitated*]: Stop it, Andrew. He'll go away. You see—he'll go away . . .

[*A long silence.* JESUS *stands dead still. The two brothers keep exchanging glances, agitated by the silent watcher. Finally* PETER *whirls round, overcome with irritation and a sort of anxiety.*]

PETER [*aggressively*]: What you staring at?

JESUS: You.
ANDREW: We've got nothing for you, friend.
PETER: So get going!

[*But* JESUS *stands looking at them, still smiling, absolutely still. They hurl out the net again, feeling a bit uncomfortable.*]

PETER: I said—what you staring at?
JESUS: You.
PETER: Well don't!
JESUS: Why not?
PETER: Makes me feel uncomfortable . . .
JESUS: Why?
PETER: What?
JESUS: Why?
PETER: You've got a cheek. I'll thump you one in a minute . . .
ANDREW: Peter—he looks like—Peter!
JESUS: You can hit me if it makes you feel more comfortable.
PETER [*exasperated*]: For God's sake . . . !
JESUS: Do not take the name of the Lord your God in vain.
PETER: Now look here—
JESUS: Do not take the name of the Lord your God in vain.

[*Pause.*]

PETER: Sorry.

[*Pause.*]

JESUS: You are a good man. And so is your brother.
ANDREW [*nervous*]: How do you know we are brothers?
JESUS: All men are brothers.

[PETER *spits.*]

You know that all men are brothers.

PETER: Only some of them work and some of them don't!

ANDREW: Some of them has swords and some of them has *wounds*.

PETER: And some of them has bread and some of them has nothing in their bellies.

[*Pause.*]

JESUS [*quietly*]: I have nothing in my belly.

PETER [*to* ANDREW]: See!

JESUS: I have been in the wilderness. For forty days and forty nights.

ANDREW: You can have a bit of my bread. Just a bit, mind . . .

JESUS: Forty days to find out—to talk with—to find out—It is *time*.

PETER: What?

JESUS: The Lord God has chosen the time. And now is the time. And now you too have been chosen.

[*To* PETER.]

What is your name?

PETER: Simon. Only I'm called Peter, if it's any of your business.

JESUS [*laughs*]: It *is* my business, Peter.

PETER: What?

JESUS: I love you, Peter.

PETER [*uncomfortable*]: What the hell are you—

JESUS: Don't be ashamed. All men should love one another. I have come to say that all over this land. *I have come!*

ANDREW: What do you mean?

JESUS: What I say.

[PETER *and* ANDREW *exchange puzzled, slightly anxious glances.*]

PETER: And where have you come from, then?

[*Pause.* JESUS *works his mouth, for the first time ill at ease.*]

Don't you know?
JESUS: Oh, yes, I know. I know.
PETER: So?
JESUS: So?
ANDREW: So where have you come from, friend? And what do you want?

[*Pause.*]

JESUS [*quietly*]: From God.
PETER [*angry*]: What did you say!
JESUS: I have come from God.

[*Silence.*]

ANDREW: We—um—
JESUS: Yes?
ANDREW: We are busy, see . . .
JESUS: What is your name?
ANDREW [*reluctantly*]: Andrew.
JESUS: I love you too, Andrew.

[PETER *laughs nervously.*]

That is funny, is it?

[*Silence.*]

Love is funny, is it?
PETER: Get off! Get away! Go on!
JESUS: You are frightened.
ANDREW: No—but you come down here from out of the blue and you—

JESUS: I told you where I come from.
ANDREW [*confused*]: Yes, but—
JESUS: I come from God. My name is Jesus and I come from God.

[PETER *almost screams with fear.*]

PETER: Get off! Go on! Leave us alone!
JESUS: Peter.
PETER: Looney! Madman! Get away!
JESUS: Peter?
PETER: You ought to be locked up—
JESUS: Peter!
PETER: —Wandering about with blood on your feet, you flaming—
ANDREW: Listen to him, Peter.
JESUS: I understand your anger and I understand your fear . . .
PETER: I'm not frightened!
ANDREW: I am. I bloody well am.
PETER: He's a looney! A looney!
JESUS: I did not want to be chosen, either. But the Kingdom of Heaven is upon us. The people are waiting. You know that. The people are waiting.
ANDREW: For the Messiah. They are waiting for the—
JESUS [*firmly*]: Yes.

[*Silence.* PETER *and* ANDREW *look at each other open-mouthed.*]

Do not be afraid.
PETER: But—listen here, you—how—how—
JESUS: I am He. I am the way.
ANDREW: No! Oh—please. No . . .
JESUS: You know that I speak the truth. They said that John the Baptist was demented. Do you believe I am demented? Do you, Peter?
PETER: Well—I—

JESUS: Look at me. Listen to me. Peter. Do you believe I am *mad*?

[PETER *stares at him. Then lowers his eyes.*]

PETER: No.

JESUS: Andrew? Do you believe I am a liar?

ANDREW: I—

JESUS: A *liar*?

ANDREW: No.

JESUS: Good. Not mad. Not a liar. Then what am I? Why do I stop you? Why are you frightened? Why does the blood pound in your head? Why does a hand touch your heart? Why does the lightning flash behind your eyes? Why is your throat so suddenly dry?

[*Pause. They stare at him. He smiles.*]

[*quietly*] Kneel down.

[*They look at each other, confused.* ANDREW *kneels, with a sob of fear:* PETER *glares at him.*]

PETER: Andrew—!

[*Then* PETER *kneels.*]

JESUS: Heavenly father. Give peace to these two brothers. Help them to be strong and give them wisdom and give them courage and give them strength.

[*Pause.*]

You may get up Peter, Andrew.

[*They get up, and cling to each other.*]

Wisdom. Strength. Courage. [*He laughs*] You will need them.

PETER: Beg pardon?

JESUS: I want you to come with me.

PETER: W-where to?

JESUS: All over this land. I must preach to the people and minister to their deepest needs. I must tell them things kept secret since the world began.

[*Pause.*]

ANDREW: How—how shall we—?

PETER: We are fishermen, my lord.

JESUS [*smiles*]: I will make you fishers of men.

[ANDREW *starts to laugh, a little nervously.*]

[*laughing*] Yes. Fishers of men.

[PETER *joins in the laughter. All three now laughing heartily. It clears the air.* JESUS *stops first.*]

You must come with me.

[*They stop laughing.*]

Leave your nets. Leave your frets and worries and daily grind. Worry no more about where your food and your clothes come from.

ANDREW: But—

JESUS: Come with me!

[*He turns to go.*]

PETER [*incredulous*]: *Now?*
JESUS: Now.

[*They hesitate.*]

[*severely*] Leave your nets, I say. The Kingdom of Heaven is upon us. And what do your nets matter when compared to *that*?

PETER: Please—it is our living.
JESUS: Through all eternity?

[*Silence.*]

Come!

[*They look at each other, then follow. Their stride quickens, and becomes almost jaunty.*]

SCENE 7

[*Outside Jerusalem. Night. A* 'BRIGAND' *(i.e. a Jewish patriot) is being crucified. The cross is raised a little, but does not soar above the crowd. A* CROWD *of Jews huddle near the cross, holding burning torches. They are kept back by three fully-accoutred* ROMAN SOLDIERS. *All is darkness except for the flicker of flames, giving the scene the necessary texture of deliberate horror. The relatives of the condemned man are nearer to the cross, and wailing in the manner now preserved by Arabs.*
After we have fully registered all that is happening, the senior Roman soldier, a CENTURION, *reads from a scroll. He does it haltingly, badly, without pomp or sonority, a soldier fulfilling an official ritual.*]

CENTURION: Joshua Bar Davidus having been condemned by his own people for contra—

[*He stumbles, unemotionally.*]

contravening the laws of his own synagogue and having been tried and condemned by Pontius Pilate, Prefect of Judaea in the Roman province of Syria under the great and awesome Emperor Tiberius, is on this day crucified for his banditry and treachery.

[*He looks up, almost bored, and gabbles.*]

Let-him-be-an-example-to-those-of-his-compatriots-who-might-be-tempted-in-their-perfidy-and-foolishness-to-behave-in-a-similar-manner. Pontius-Pilate-Prefect-of-Judaea.

[*The man on the cross begins to scream. A low, wretched moan comes from the onlookers.*]

CROWD: De-liv-er us! De-liv-er us . . .

[*The condemned man continues to gurgle. The* CENTURION *shuts his eyes for half a second, more in irritation than compassion.*]

CENTURION: Soldier!
SOLDIER: Sir?
CENTURION: Finish the job.
SOLDIER: But he ent hung up there no more than an hour, sir.
CENTURION [*bored*]: Do you want to listen to that noise all night?

[SOLDIER *shrugs.*]

SOLDIER: 'Sall the same to me, sir. I'm not bothered.

CENTURION: I'm not bothered, soldier! I'm *bored*. [*hastily*] Finish the job, I say!

[*The screaming stops with a low gurgle. The* CROWD *lower their eyes and then drop to their knees, virtually in unison.*]

[*shouts*] There's one more Messiah to put in a grave in Golgotha! Superstitious fools! Go home! *Go home!*

SCENE 8

[*The hills in Judaea. Though not a part of this scene, the crucified 'terrorist' is left hanging on the cross.* PETER, ANDREW, JAMES *and* JOHN *are sitting in the semi-darkness, round a fire of sticks.* PETER *is baking some dough, twisted round a stick and held into the fire.*]

ANDREW: Isn't it done yet? I'm starving—
PETER: Wait!
JAMES: When he came to me yesterday I—
ANDREW [*laughs*]: You didn't think it would be like this.
PETER: Ow! This is bloody hot . . .
JAMES: No. I didn't think it would be like—where is he? What is he doing?
PETER: Praying. Here, James, have some of this—
JAMES: Thanks. Praying?
ANDREW [*firmly*]: Talking to God.
JOHN: Is he? Is he?
PETER: Here, have some. Is he what?
JOHN: Is he—*talking*. To God.

[JAMES *is rather forlorn.*]

JAMES: He *said* he was from God. I laughed. I mean, I wanted to laugh. Did you laugh? John?
JOHN: No. I started to hit out, to—to hit *at* him and—

[*Pause.*]

JAMES: Yes?
JOHN: And he kissed me.

[*Silence. They chew on the twists of bread.*]

JAMES: I don't know . . .
PETER [*mouth full*]: You don't know what?
JAMES [*shouts*]: *I don't know what I'm doing here!*

[*Silence.*]

PETER: Go home, then.
JAMES: What?
PETER: Go home. Go on, James.
JAMES: Is he really talking to God. I mean, is he—?
ANDREW: Oh, not you and all!

[*Silence.*]

PETER: Simple. It's very simple. You either believe him or not.

[*Silence.*]

ANDREW: He *is* talking to God. He *is*. He *is*!

[*Silence.* JAMES *gets up.*]

JOHN: Are you—?

PETER [*angrily*]: Sit down!
JAMES: I'm going to see. *I've got to see.* I've got to be sure . . .
ANDREW: Come back! James!

[*They look at each other.* JAMES *goes behind the big rock. Silence. A long, tense silence.*]

PETER [*hisses*]: Fool . . . bloody, bloody fool . . .

[*And* JAMES *comes back. He hurls himself on to the ground, by the fire, his face hidden.*]

JOHN: What—?
ANDREW [*for himself*]: He *was* talking to God. He was. He was!
JOHN [*whisper*]: Was he? James?

[JAMES *raises his head, a sob in his voice.*]

JAMES: He—
PETER: Shut up.
JAMES: He was—He was—
PETER: Why don't you go home!
JOHN [*frightened*]: He was *what*?
JAMES [*wails*]: He—was—being—SICK!

[*Silence. A horrible silence, except for* JAMES, *who is sobbing.* JOHN *is the first to take decisive action. He gets up, brushing himself down.* PETER *and* ANDREW *look at him, then at each other.*]

PETER [*gritting his teeth*]: Had enough? Already?
JOHN: When he kissed me, I—

[*He makes a helpless little gesture.*]

33

ANDREW [*desperate*]: Stay—oh, please—please stay—

JOHN: But *why*? What are we *doing*? There he is—we think he's talking to God and—instead he's heaving up his guts—it—it—

[JAMES *lifts his head from his arms. He stares at* JOHN, *registering what is happening.*]

JAMES: No! *No!*

[JOHN *stops, astounded.*]

JOHN: But you said—you—

JAMES: Oh, no. He—

[*He cannot get the words out.*]

He was in —pain. Terrible pain.

[*Silence.*]

[*faltering*] He was choking on bile and—and—blood.

ANDREW [*softly*]: Oh, Jesus. Poor Jesus.

JAMES: And as I looked—as I—he—I saw him topple into his own spew.

[*Silence.*]

JOHN: But look here . . .

JAMES [*sobbing*]: And—and he looked straight in front of him. He didn't look *up*. Not *up*. Just straight in front of him—and —like it was you or me he was talking to—he said 'Father—please. Father. Let me be *just a man.*'

[*Pause.*]

I will follow him to the ends of the earth.

[*The light fades. A spotlight picks out the crucified man, still hanging on cross.*]

SCENE 9

[*The Temple in Jerusalem.* CAIAPHAS *is in debate with two* ELDERS. *In the background we still see the crucified man hanging on the cross.*]

CAIAPHAS: A sheep cannot argue with the walls of his pen and a goat cannot rub his horns against the clouds. We must see the situation as it really *is*. That is our dilemma.

1ST PRIEST: But Caiaphas, we are men, the leaders of Israel. Not sheep or goats, bleating their way to the milk pail or the slaughter house. We *must* defy the Romans.

2ND PRIEST: Or at least we in the Temple must not give the *appearance* of being *too* ready to co-operate with the civil power. I fear that this is what our people think.

[*Pause.*]

CAIAPHAS: Do the Roman soldiers enter the Temple?

2ND PRIEST: No, Master.

CAIAPHAS: Have they taken the money of the Temple?

1ST PRIEST: It was threatened. To meet the cost of the aqueduct.

CAIAPHAS: But have they *taken it*?

2ND PRIEST: No.

CAIAPHAS: Do they now bring their standards unhooded into the Holy City?

2ND PRIEST: No.

CAIAPHAS: Do they prevent by force of arms the performance of any religious ceremony or ritual?

1ST PRIEST: No. Not yet.

CAIAPHAS: Well then!

1ST PRIEST: But the people are not satisfied with such tokens. They look to us for courage, and cunning, and defiance.

2ND PRIEST: Most of all defiance.

CAIAPHAS: Are we men of realism and caution for the sake of our faith—or are we wild Zealots and misguided dreamers who would reduce Jerusalem to ashes and sacrifice our people in the name of a political ideal which is not, has not been, and will not for many a long year be within our grasp?

[*Silence. He has spoken with great finger-jabbing vigour.* CAIAPHAS *looks up and around. His voice is suddenly thick with emotion.*]

This our Temple, our solace, our joy, our heart. It will stand a thousand years. Yes. And another thousand after that. Soldiers come and go. Prefects and governors and generals and orators will agitate the world all the while. But they too will be as nothing while the Temple stands, the glory of our people, who know the true God and will never deny it, come flame or pestilence or sword.

[*Sudden spurt of contempt.*]

Or a Prefect called Pontius Pilate with the manners of a carpenter and the intellect of a wood beetle!

[*He turns to them, imploringly.*]

I co-operate with the Prefect because I am more clever than he is. I co-operate with the Prefect because he has more

soldiers than I have. I co-operate with the Prefect because I
have God and he is a heathen.

2ND PRIEST [*hesitant*]: But our people have not forgotten the
man John. Their talk is all of him, and of—the Messiah.

1ST PRIEST: The streets are thick with rumour. There is a mood
of rebellion in the air. We cannot shut our ears to it any
longer.

2ND PRIEST: You must listen to the people!

1ST PRIEST [*urgently*]: The Messiah, master! The Messiah!

[*A long pause.* CAIAPHAS *picks at a thread in his sleeve.*]

CAIAPHAS [*quietly*]: Two men who blasphemously claimed to be
the Christ were executed yesterday. God did not step down
and pluck them off the cross.

[*Behind them, the body on the cross is taken down from the cross by
Roman levies, and thrown roughly into a handcart.*]

SCENE 10

[PONTIUS PILATE's *residence.* PILATE *is hearing a military report
of some importance. He is slightly agitated, aware of all the fever
in the air.*]

PILATE [*plaintively*]: But I thought it was only the Jews who
were awaiting the Messiah!

COMMANDER: No, Prefect. Also the Samaritans between Judaea
and Galilee. They too wait for a Messiah.

PILATE: But—look here—

COMMANDER [*firmly*]: The Samaritans have the same disease, Sir!

PILATE [*protesting*]: The Jews and the Samaritans spit upon one another! They hate each other to the very worms in their bellies.

COMMANDER: The Samaritans claim to be the descendants of the original Israelites.

[PILATE *waves his hands in despair.*]

PILATE: That's an honour?

COMMANDER: This whole land rings with the names of Moses and Joshua and other tribesmen from the dim and distant past.

PILATE: Ye Gods. These people—it is as though the worms laid claim to the earth because of their proximity to it!

COMMANDER: Anyway, sir—the point is—

PILATE: Trouble. The point is *always* trouble.

COMMANDER [*tight-lipped*]: No trouble that we cannot put down.

PILATE: Insurrection?

COMMANDER: Insurrection.

PILATE [*sighs*]: Cunning priests and a demented population. *Where* is it *now*?

COMMANDER: The Samaritans are in the grip of a particularly feverish Messianic movement, according to our intelligence.

PILATE: There are more Messiahs in these few sour acres than there are flies in a peasant's larder.

COMMANDER [*briskly*]: Quite. Swot them before they lay their eggs.

[PILATE *stares at him, then laughs.*]

PILATE: Very good. Very good . . .

COMMANDER [*impatiently*]: The Samaritans are being stirred up by a prophet who says he can reveal the hiding place of some so-called sacred vessels hidden by this—um—this Moses.

PILATE: And?

COMMANDER: They are gathering by the hundred at Mount Gerizim.

PILATE [*correcting the pronunciation*]: Gerizim.

[*They lean over the maps.*]

COMMANDER: Good terrain. For them. As good as a fortress.
PILATE: Armed? Are they?
COMMANDER: Oh yes. And as wild as hornets.
PILATE: Ye Gods.
COMMANDER [*dryly*]: No—only one God, apparently. These people, Jew or Samaritan, are not very well endowed with imagination.
PILATE: But they fight well.
COMMANDER: They fight, all right.

[*Pause.*]

PILATE: Take all the men from Caesarea except the immediate Palace Guard.
COMMANDER [*pleased*]: Sir!
PILATE: Put them down. And put them down hard.
COMMANDER: Sir!
PILATE: All prisoners will be executed.

[*Slight pause.*]

COMMANDER [*less enthused*]: Sir.

[PILATE *looks at him.*]

PILATE: Once and for all, perhaps, we can exorcise this tedious ghost.
COMMANDER: Sir?
PILATE [*irritably*]: The Messiah, man. The bloody Messiah!

39

SCENE 11

[*A track into Caesarea. The* SAMARITAN PRISONERS *are arriving. In initial darkness, we hear the chant of the beaten Samaritans—a low, murmuring, rhythmic chant.*]

PRISONERS: Moses! De-liv-er us. Moses! De-liv-er us! De-liv-er us! Moses! Mo-ses! Deliver us!

[*The lights go up to show files of* PRISONERS *coming through auditorium. They are whipped and driven by* ROMAN SOLDIERS *in very aggressive mood. They kick at the file, brutally. They reach the stage. At the front of the stage a* SAMARITAN PRISONER *collapses on to his knees, totally exhausted.*]

PRISONER: Water . . . oh water . . .

[*The nearest* ROMAN SOLDIER *signals down the line to his companion.*]

GUARD: Here's one as has had it! Legius!

[*He starts beating the* SAMARITAN *with his short truncheon-like club. The file shuffles on, off stage. Their chant recedes.* LEGIUS *comes back to help. The two* ROMAN SOLDIERS *systematically beat the* SAMARITAN *to death. They do not speak or smile as they do it. The murder is entirely routine and matter of fact. The man's initial screams become gurgles, and then are silent. He is dragged away, a raw, pulped, broken and bloody mess. The stage is left bare, and quiet.*]

SCENE 12

[*The hills of Judah.* JESUS *is preaching. His audience is the theatre audience. Behind* JESUS *stand* PETER, ANDREW, JAMES *and* JOHN, *ranged along the stage.* JESUS *is, as it were, in full flight, as though he has been speaking for some time. His physical strength and charisma have obviously grown. He speaks with a tremendous urgency, right at the audience, bouncing his remarks off them, sometimes still, sometimes jigging on the balls of his feet: a natural orator.*]

JESUS: An eye for an eye! A tooth for a tooth!

PETER: Hit them hard!

JAMES: Hit them fast!

JESUS: A life for a life!

ANDREW: Bone for bone!

JOHN: Muscle for muscle!

PETER: Sword for sword!

JESUS: Kick for kick!

JOHN: Blow for blow!

ANDREW: Sting for sting!

PETER: Head for head!

JAMES: Corpse for corpse!

JESUS: An eye for an eye. A tooth for a tooth. Is that not so? Is that not our way?

FOUR DISCIPLES: Yes! Yes!

JESUS: Yes! So our forefathers have spoken. So the world has always spoken. So it speaks *now*. Look around! An eye for an eye. A tooth for a tooth. Look around! And they have also said love your kinsman—right? Makes sense! Love your compatriot. Love your own kind. And *hate* the enemy. HATE-your-enemy. Right?

FOUR DISCIPLES: HATE!

JESUS: Hate your enemy. But love your own kind. Your own sort of people. Your own crowd.

41

[Slight pause. He steps forward.]

Let us be cosy. You have come together here in this place. You have things in common. Oh, cosy, cosy people. You are *safe* here. The world may be falling apart. Soldiers may be waiting. Heads are breaking. But not now. Not here. It's *all right* here. Calm here. Safe here. Cosy here . . . So go on—touch each other. *[he laughs]* Come on—the person next to you. Man or woman. Touch! Touch! Go on. Don't be frightened. Go with the flow. Don't hold back. Hold each other by the hand. Yes. That's it. All of you. Go on. Hold each other by the hand. You there—yes, you too! It's nice. Oh, very nice. Love, love, love. There—you see. You see! Shhh! Don't be shy. Hold each other. Touch each other. *Caress* each other. Hand to hand. Twine your fingers. Lock your hands. See? Eeeasy! Right? Eh? Easy! It's *easy* to love your brother. Here you all are, collected together in one place. *Easy. Easy* to love only those who are like you. Why—even the tax collectors can do that!

[Laughter, and some applause.]

But what—tell me then, dear, safe, cosy, smug people—*what* is so extraordinary about holding the hands of your own brothers and sisters? Mmm?

[His voice begins to grate.]

Do you want me to *congratulate* you for loving those who love you? Eh? Eh?

[Silence.]

Love your enemies.

[*Pause.*]

Love your enemies! Yes. I say it again. Love your enemies. It is all that is left to us. It is all that can save us. Love—the hardest, toughest, most challenging, most invincible *force* of all. Love your enemies. Love those who hate you. Love those who would destroy you. Love the man who would kick you and spit at you. Love the soldier who drives his sword into your belly. Love the brigand who robs and tortures you. Love your enemies.

[*Pause.*]

[*moved*] Listen to me. I want you to listen to me. What I am saying to you now has not been said since the world began. If you do as I say, if you act upon my teaching, then you will see the Kingdom of Heaven here too on earth! I bring you the answer. I bring you the way. I am holding up a light in the darkness. Listen! Oh, brothers, sisters, *listen to me!*

[*He is almost whispering, and all but in tears.*]

The good Lord God makes the same sun shine on the good and the bad, the rich and the poor. The same rain wets the heads of the honest and the dishonest, the exploiters and the exploited. We cannot divide ourselves. We must love one another or we must die. That is a fact. Do *not* take an eye for an eye or a tooth for a tooth. No!

[*He speaks with more vigour.*]

Do *not* set yourself against the man who does you wrong. No! If he hits you—ah, but what then you say? What about that, then? Well—if he hits you on the right cheek, turn and offer him the left cheek.

43

[JESUS *stops, smiling, playing with his audience.*]

Yes—it will hurt twice as much, my friends!

[*Laughter.*]

PETER: Especially if I was to do it, Master!

[*Renewed laughter.*]

JESUS: Or if a Roman soldier was to do it—?

[*Laughter stops.*]

[*quietly*] Then turn the other cheek. Turn the other cheek.

[*Fractional pause.*]

Pray for your enemy. *Love* your persecutor. How in the end can he be changed? Those who kill the persecutor *become* persecutors. The exploited become the exploiters. Today's friend may be tomorrow's enemy. What salvation is there! What sense is there in all this? *It is easy—eeeasy—to love only those who love you.* Would *I* come to tell you easy things? Do you *want* me to tell you easy things? Are you not the generation that is waiting for the sign? *Are you not the generation that may be the last on earth?* Are you not they who must make straight the path? Oh, I tell you it is hard to follow me. Hard, hard to get the poison out of your veins. For I say to you love your persecutors. What else is there? I say to you that if a man in authority orders you to walk a mile—then walk two miles! What can he do? His authority is doubly mocked. If a man sues you for your coat—then give him the shirt off your back as well! Oh, lawyers. *Poor* lawyers. What-will-they-do?

[*laughs*] Do not judge your brother. Let him out of the prison. Oh, policemen. *Poor* policemen. What-will-they-do? [*laughs*] It is hard what I say. Hard to do. And hard to *understand*. You will have to be better men than your leaders before you can make the Kingdom of Heaven. Give when you are asked to give. And then you can ask, too. Forgive so that you yourselves can be forgiven. I know it is hard. I know. And your spirits are oppressed. Your minds rot in your bodies. You are fenced in by fear. Fear. You fear those who are not like you. You *refuse* to love them. And so they *refuse* to love you. Oh, world. *Poor* world. What-will-it-do? Is justice only for the strong? So it seems, so it seems. Will the big always beat the little, the rich always feed off the poor? So it seems, so it seems.

But listen—oh, listen. *Blessed* are the poor, for they shall see the Kingdom of Heaven. The rich are thieves. They *must* be. And *blessed* are those who sorrow, for they shall be comforted. Blessed are the meek—the ones you despise. The earth will belong to them. Blessed are those who hunger and thirst to see justice—for justice, real justice, they *shall* see. When? But when— when—*when*? When you heed what I say! Blessed are those that show mercy, mercy will be shown to them. Blessed are the pure in heart, for they shall see God. Blessed are the peacemakers, they are the children of God. Blessed are those who suffer for the cause of right, for theirs is the Kingdom of God. Set your minds on that. On God's kingdom and God's justice. Never mind about money. That is just another word for hate. Another word for murder. Another word for war. So never mind about *money*. You cannot love money and love God. You cannot love money and love your fellow man. And your fellow man *is* God. Where else is God? You cannot serve God *and* money! You cannot! Think of what that means. Think of all the wars and prisons and starvation and sickness and suffering and exploitation—when are you going to stop it? When are you going to change it? When are you going

45

to *change*? But where else will change begin except *in you*. In buildings? In institutions? In prisons? In battles? In *hate*? No. No, no, no. Begin here. Begin now. Open your minds. See the world as it might be, as it could be. Treat others as you would like them to treat you. Ask and you will receive. Seek and you will find. Knock and the door will open. Now? This very moment? Yes, now, if you will begin. With love. Not easy love. Not simple love. But the hard kind. The kind that changes the world, that blunts the sword, that topples the giant, that empties the prisons, that makes money useless. The hardest love of all. The love which hurts. Love for your enemies. That is what I have come to tell you. Will you listen? Oh, will you? Will you? *Love your enemy.* Love—your— enemy!

END OF ACT ONE

ACT TWO

SCENE 1

[PILATE's *residence. A Roman after dinner entertainment is taking place. Two battle-scarred* 'BOXERS' *with leather thongs across their knuckles, bleeding and gasping for breath, are warily circling each other.* PILATE, *his wife* PROCLA, *the* COMMANDER *and other* ROMANS, *their cups constantly replenished by servants, are watching the contest.* PROCLA *clearly does not greatly care for such entertainment. But* PILATE *is glowing with enthusiasm. One of the* 'BOXERS' *lands a bone-cracking blow. The other sags heavily, but manages to stay on his feet.* PILATE *claps his hands.*]

PILATE: Oh very good! Very good!
COMMANDER: Not good enough to put the man down, sir.

[*Silence. From the* BOXERS *come groans, grunts, thuds: a merciless fight.*]

PILATE: They are propping each other up! Come on! *Come—on!*
PROCLA: Why cannot we listen to a singer instead, Pontius?

[*But he takes no notice, entirely absorbed in the contest.*]

PILATE: Excellent! An excellent blow—!
COMMANDER: The decider, I think. He's got him now . . .

[*One of the two contestants is obviously about to be beaten to the floor. He gropes desperately at the other's thighs, trying to stay up.*]

PROCLA: We are surrounded by a people with a genius for story and song, an ancient and beautiful culture, and yet we have to watch—

[*But she stops in fascinated horror. The weaker* BOXER *collapses and the other straddles over him.* PILATE *rises, shouting and screaming.*]

PILATE: Finish him off! Finish the job, man!

[*The victor clasps his fists together like a hammer and crashes them down on the neck of the fallen* BOXER. *A hiss of release from the on-lookers. The flame dies on* PILATE. *Standing, arms raised, he is aware that he has momentarily compromised his dignity.*]

[*sighs*] Why do I always get so excited? Why?

PROCLA: It is not good for you.

47

PILATE: There is—a sort of beauty in the struggle itself—

COMMANDER: If they are evenly enough matched, sir.

PILATE: But the kill—no. Then there is nothing. Then it is just brutish.

COMMANDER: The kill is the point of it.

PROCLA: Then it is *without* point!

PILATE: No, no. The *struggle* is the point of it. The conclusion is an irrelevance. Like life itself. You dream, you scheme, you eat, you drink, you love then—phut! Nothing! A blackness after the pain.

PROCLA: You see—it makes you gloomy. Such violence makes you gloomy.

PILATE [*irritated*]. Violence?

COMMANDER: It is a sport, ma'am.

[*The beaten* BOXER *is being dragged away by the legs.* PILATE *is watching.*]

PILATE: A sport.

[*He says it with a dull, mechanical voice.*]

A sport. A pastime. A mere diversion.

PROCLA: Brutish.

COMMANDER: Both men were prisoners, ma'am.

PROCLA: It is still brutish.

[*Pause.* PILATE *sighs heavily.*]

Why do we not have song or dance or story or—

PILATE [*interrupting*]: My *dear* wife! Violence you call it? Violence is what brought us here. Violence is what feeds and clothes you! Do you want to tuck it away—not to see it, or acknowledge it—or what?

PROCLA: I prefer song.
PILATE: She prefers song!

[*The* COMMANDER *laughs.*]

[*cuttingly*] As would any civilised being.

[*The* COMMANDER *bites off his laugh.*]

PROCLA: We are amongst an old and beautiful culture.
PILATE: Old and beautiful and *wilful*.
COMMANDER: They sing all right. And then try to strangle you!
PROCLA: Have you *heard* their songs and stories?

[*Pause.*]

PILATE: Yes. They—*humiliate* us. Yes. I've heard them.

[*Pause.*]

PROCLA: The songs of Zion.
PILATE: I know, I know.
PROCLA: 'If I take the wings of the morning, and dwell in the uttermost parts of the sea; even there shall thy hand lead me, and thy right hand shall hold me.'

[*Pause.*]

PILATE [*with an edge to his voice*]: 'Let the high praises of God be in their mouth, and a two-edged sword in their hand; To execute vengeance upon the heathen and punishments upon the people; to bind their kings with chains, and their nobles with fetters of iron.'

[*Pause.*]

49

PROCLA: All people sing of war.

PILATE: But *this* people know who they are. They have an identity which cannot be destroyed, and they cannot be cowed.

COMMANDER: Show them a lance and they will run!

PILATE: *That*, sir, is mere prudence.

COMMANDER: All I know is they are a troublesome lot, waiting for a leader to foment treachery and insurrection.

CAPTAIN: Our soldiers sense it, sir. They feel it on their patrols, and they don't like it.

PROCLA: A Messiah.

PILATE: Oh, that word!

COMMANDER [*dryly*]: The latest contender for the position is a madman from—um—Nazareth, sir.

PROCLA: A carpenter.

PILATE [*quickly*]: How do you know this?

[*She shrugs.*]

PROCLA: The servants talk.

CAPTAIN: That is so, sir. A carpenter.

PILATE: Then he can start making his own cross! Eh? Eh?

[*Laughter.* PILATE *is pleased with his joke.*]

COMMANDER: But—well, this one is a bit different, sir. According to our reports.

PILATE: Different? You mean—he is not of the Zealot party?

COMMANDER: He goes around preaching peace.

[*Pause.*]

PILATE: Why does there seem to be *contempt* in your voice, Commander?

COMMANDER: 'Love your enemies', that seems to be his war-cry.

[*He sniggers. Some laughter.*]

PILATE [*carefully*]: And he includes the Romans in this?
COMMANDER [*sniffs*]: Apparently so.
PILATE [*thoughtful*]: Mmm. Love your enemies. Love your—?
And they *listen* to this?
CAPTAIN: Great crowds, sir.
COMMANDER: But only out in the hills. Nothing to worry us.
PILATE [*puzzled*]: Love your *enemies*?
PROCLA: I have been told that the people in the villages believe
him to be from their God.
COMMANDER: Then their God has seen sense at last!

[*Some laughter. But* PILATE *does not join in.*]

PILATE [*self-absorbed*]: Love your enemies. Love—your enemies?
PROCLA: Pontius? What are you thinking?

[*Pause.*]

PILATE: I am thinking that the Jews know only too well that they
cannot drive us out by force of arms.
COMMANDER: Not in a million years!
PILATE [*in a rising tone*]: I am thinking that they know we are
stupid as well as strong.

[*The* COMMANDER *turns his head away.*]

Great crowds? And you, Procla—you too have heard
of this? The servants talk of it—*here. Love your enemies.* What
would we do with their love?
PROCLA [*eagerly*]: Return it.

[PILATE *slaps his knee, hard.*]

PILATE: And put down our swords! By the Gods, Commander—
a madman, you say? Nothing to worry us?

COMMANDER[*firmly*]: Harmless, sir. Quite harmless. He does not
come into the cities.

[PROCLA *is trying to work something out.*]

PROCLA[*puzzled*]: But what does it mean? If you really think about
it—no, it doesn't make . . . Love your enemies? What on earth
does it *mean*?

COMMANDER: Pardon me, ma'am. But it means that the man is a
lunatic!

[*Roars of laughter. But* PILATE *does not join in. The laughter ebbs as
eyes turn to* PILATE.]

PILATE: The two-edged sword.

SCENE 2

[*The Temple in Jerusalem. Candles light the lofty interior, sending
great bouncing shadows leaping around the walls. It is echoey and
feels awesome and sanctified.* CAIAPHAS *speaks slowly, and his words
almost reverberate through the building. He is addressing five of the
so-called Temple police—laymen who enforce the 'Law' of Judaism,
the words of the Prophets.*]

CAIAPHAS [*slowly*]: I would sooner be torn slowly limb from
limb, or nailed up on the cross, or plunged into the brimstone
fires of hell than allow blasphemy to rot at the foundations of
our faith and our being. Now you are the police of the Temple
and as such the guardians of the Law of the Holy Prophets.

You have to be my eyes and ears and, if necessary, my finger of accusation. Our people are confused, unhappy, gullible and tormented now. They await signs from heaven, and so charlatans or maniacs or misguided simpletons or vengeful Zealots are more than ready to give them signs from heaven.

JUDAS ISCARIOT: But, master, what if there *should* be such signs? Supposing—

CAIAPHAS [*angrily*]: And, Judas Iscariot, do you not suppose that *I* should know of them?

[*Pause.*]

JUDAS: I am sorry, master. I—

[CAIAPHAS *smiles gently, and holds up his hand.*]

CAIAPHAS: I know, Judas. I understand you. These are hard times. We can almost feel the marrow rotting in our bones and the spirit choking in our throats. All of us need a sign from God. There are alien soldiers in the streets. There is sickness. There are the executions of patriots. There is doubt and grief and panic stinking like sewage in our towns and villages. Surely— we say—surely God has not abandoned us?

JUDAS: Oh, master. God will never abandon us.

CAIAPHAS: No, Judas.

JUDAS: So now is perhaps the moment when—

CAIAPHAS [*firmly, interrupting*]: The moment when we shall be *tested* by our Lord God.

ALL: Amen.

CAIAPHAS: When our forefathers fled from Egypt—did God abandon them?

ALL: He parted the waters.

CAIAPHAS: When Jericho stood stone-walled in the path of the Promised Land—did God abandon Joshua?

ALL: The walls fell down.

CAIAPHAS: And nor did God abandon us when our people were carried off in captivity to Babylon. Our people sat down by the rivers of Babylon and they hung their harps in the trees and, yes, they wept when they remembered Zion. And so now, too, they weep. But God did not abandon them in the days of old and so He will not abandon us now.

ALL: Amen.

CAIAPHAS: But our God is a jealous God. And he will not be mocked. Not by soldiers. And not by tramps and madmen and —carpenters either.

[*Pause.*]

JUDAS [*carefully*]: The carpenter is a man whom in all conscience one could—*love.*

[*Pause.*]

CAIAPHAS: Judas.

JUDAS: Master?

CAIAPHAS: Does he tell the people to obey their priests?

[JUDAS *lowers his head.*]

Or does he not say that unless they show themselves to be [*harshly*] better men than the doctors of the law, they will not enter the Kingdom of Heaven? Answer me?

JUDAS: He—yes, he does say something like that, master . . .

CAIAPHAS [*scornfully*]: *Something* like that?

JUDAS: Yes, master. It is an impertinence.

CAIAPHAS: An impertinence! To say who will and who will not enter the Kingdom of Heaven!

[JUDAS *is silent.*]

And does he not say that Elijah has already come? In the shape of the wild man John?

JUDAS: He—implies it, master.

CAIAPHAS [*angrily*]: And so implies that he, the carpenter's son from Nazareth is, God forgive me, the Messiah!

JUDAS: He loves the poor.

CAIAPHAS: The rich are unlovable.

JUDAS: He cures the sick.

CAIAPHAS: And just as many people are buried in the ground.

JUDAS: He speaks—powerfully, and convincingly.

CAIAPHAS: So does a man who wants to sell you a carpet.

JUDAS [*almost in tears*]: And he tells the people to love their enemies.

CAIAPHAS [*hisses*]: He tells them *what*?

JUDAS [*faltering*]: To—love—their enemies . . .

CAIAPHAS: What did Joshua and the Israelites do to the people of Jericho?

[*Pause. Shouts.*]

Well?

JUDAS: Killed every man, woman and child in the city.

CAIAPHAS: And what did our God do to the Egyptians? To their first born?

[JUDAS *buries his face in his hands.*]

[*quietly*] Oh Judas, Judas. I love the gentleness in your soul. Come, do not weep.

JUDAS: I am sorry, master.

CAIAPHAS: How shall we as a people chosen of God survive if we kiss the sword that would slay us? How shall we defend our faith and the one true God if we do not hate His enemies and struggle for survival?

JUDAS: But, master—

CAIAPHAS: Enough!

JUDAS: Is it not possible that this Jesus is indeed the Messiah?

[CAIAPHAS *is about to shout an angry denial, but stops, and smiles.*]

CAIAPHAS: It is—when all is said and done, extremely improbable.

JUDAS: Improbable, yes, but—

CAIAPHAS: But not impossible? Well, we shall see. We shall see. Meanwhile I have made clear to you all what I expect, what I *demand* of you.

ALL: Yes master.

CAIAPHAS: Invite this Jesus to show you a sign from heaven. Invite him to give his full support to the doctors of the law and to the prophets. Ask him what we should do about the Romans. Follow him and listen to him and observe him and debate with him and note down any of his blasphemies. Judas, you may be right. You may. You, at least, will find no difficulty in becoming to all intents and purposes one of the man's raggle-taggle disciples.

JUDAS: No, no difficulty. Master.

[*Slight pause.*]

CAIAPHAS [*severely*]: Just so long as you also find and continue to find no difficulty in recognising the spiritual authority of the Temple, the sanctity of the law and the prophets and the rightful and jealous and terrible claims of the Lord your God. Watch your path, Judas Iscariot. Do not stumble into the filthy ditch of blasphemy!

SCENE 3

[JESUS *and the four* APOSTLES *are sprawled, resting, on the grass of a hillside near a village where he has just preached. Behind them, a cross—empty, almost unnoticed. Just an ordinary, accepted part of the landscape. They are passing round a gourd of wine.* PETER, *drinking too greedily, slurps some down his chin.*]

JESUS: Peter! Don't be so greedy!

PETER: I'm sorry Master. [*breaks wind*] It's just that I've got more to fill than the rest of you . . .

JESUS [*amused*]: Well, I'm thirsty too you know—*who* did all the talking? Eh?

[ANDREW *passes* JESUS *the wine. He drinks, smacking his lips with satisfaction.*]

ANDREW: They liked it, Master. I was watching their eyes.

JESUS: Always watch their eyes, Andrew. When they film over with boredom, start to tell them a story.

JOHN: Yes! I like the one about the traveller who fell among thieves, and the Samaritan.

JESUS [*eagerly*]: Do you think they understood? Was I making myself clear to them?

ALL: Yes . . . oh, yes . . .

[*But* JESUS, *introspective, turns in on himself.*]

JESUS: I don't know . . . I'm not so sure about that . . .

JOHN: The crowds are getting bigger. All the time.

JAMES: More and more of our people are talking about you and arguing about you—

PETER: They've laughed and they've cried.

ANDREW: And gone home with their heads singing with new thoughts.

JESUS: I don't know. I don't know.

PETER: Beats fishing, any road.

[*He sniggers.*]

JESUS [*angrily*]: What did you say?

PETER [*defensive*]: Well, you know what I mean—journeying around the country like this, seeing all sorts of people and big crowds and . . .

JESUS: You enjoy it, do you?

[*There is such a bite in the question that* PETER *gapes back at him confused.*]

I said—you *enjoy* it, do you?

PETER: I like being with *you* my Lord . . . ?

[*Agitated,* JESUS *stands up, towering above them.*]

JESUS: Fun! That's what it is to all of you—a jaunt through the countryside, living only for today and not the morrow . . .

[*They are making protesting noises.*]

Shut up! Shut up! Before I lose my patience with all of you! What do you think I am? *Who* do you think I am?

[*He strides about among them, extremely agitated.*]

Yes, the people listen. Yes, more of them are coming out to meet us. Yes, I can move and excite them, to pity or terror. Yes, the days pass with some hope and some gain. But great God in Heaven have I come for *this*? To *pass the time*! [*he snorts*] Why do we skulk about on the hillsides and in the sad little villages? Eh? Where are the Temple police, then? The Romans? Eh? I must go to the Holy City itself. Into the Temple. Clear out the pigs and the profiteers. Make them see who—*Who am I?*

[*To himself, he repeats it, almost doubtingly.*]

Who-am-I?

JAMES: Lord—?

[*He begins to sweep on, twitching with excitement.*]

JESUS: You must go on ahead of me, each of you. You must
announce when I am to speak, where I am to speak. You must
make the water ripple. And—listen!—from now on my friends,
my dear friends, from now on we—*trumpet* our coming.
We speak loudly. And clearly. We are here to cleanse a whole
nation with the purity of the One who is on high. Ach—
the light must not be hidden! The truth must not be whispered!

[*He ruffles* PETER'*s hair.*]

Then, my Peter, you can rightly be filled with joy and exult-
ation!

PETER: Yes, master.

JESUS: Why! They don't even know *who I am* in their palaces
and temples and garrisons. I do not challenge them out *here*
in the sour grass!

JOHN: Your words have spread far, Jesus. You have—

[JESUS *waves him down almost contemptuously.*]

JESUS: A few miles. A few villages. Along the shores of Galilee!

JOHN: Yes—but—

JESUS: And I want my words to echo along the edges of the whole
world! The whole wide world—do you hear me? Eh? Or else
I might as well be making tables and benches in a carpenter's
workshop . . .

[JESUS *goes to the cross. He almost strokes at the wood, his expression
suddenly less tormented.*]

59

Good timber, this. Hewed with the grain from the heart of the tree. I could fill a room with tables and chairs with wood like this.

[*He chops the air with his hand.*]

Cha-ow! Split, it would, straight as ever you could want. Yes! There's nothing like a bit of wood in your hands. Cha-ow! Not a knot in it, see? Good stuff.

[*He puts his head against the cross, as though it were a pillow, and momentarily closes his eyes.*]

[*whispers*] Father . . . Father . . .

[*His shoulders start to shake, as though in sobbing.* ANDREW *steps forward anxiously to comfort him, putting his hands on* JESUS' *shoulders.*]

ANDREW: Oh, Master, please . . .

[*But* JESUS *turns swiftly, and we see that, far from sobbing, he is in fact shaking with laughter.*]

JUDAS: Wh-what is it?
JESUS: A tree! A t-tut-tree!

[*He laughs out loud, then speaks, still smiling.*]

God puts it in the soil. A tiny little seed. He sends the sun to warm it. He sends the rain to feed it. He lets the earth hug the little plant like a mother with a baby. So it grows. Years and years it grows. Little roots like veins twisting underneath our feet. First it's a sapling, tossed by the wind, a feeble thing. But still sun, rain, still it grows. And grows. Oh, a huge thing.

A great, strong tower climbing towards heaven. Older now than a man, than two men. What has it not seen? Eh?

PETER [*child-like*]: Go on—go on!

JESUS: Cha-ow! Down it comes! Crash! Oh, great tree, brought low by the axe. Eh? But God doesn't mind—

JUDAS [*aloof, still*]: Doesn't he? How do *you*—?

JESUS: No-oo. What are trees for? Wood. God wants us to build. To have tables to eat off. Chairs to sit on. He has filled the earth with good things, all for man, for me, for you. So He doesn't mind, does He? No-oo. All that sun. All that rain. All those years. All that struggle from seed to giant—well, tables and chairs are fine things too! But look what we do. Look! A cross! To kill a man! All that sun. All that rain. And here is the end of it—something to hold up and stretch out a man while he dies!

[*Again, he throws back his head and laughs. The others are puzzled, and even rather disapproving.*]

JOHN: But what is funny about that, Lord?

JESUS: Man!

ANDREW: What?

JESUS [*angry rhetoric*]: Man! That's what is *funny* about it! Man, silly, stupid, murdering man! We take the good things God gave us in order to *hurt* each other! Why—look at us!—Look around you, here in this dreadful place. And think. Look into the distance, at that haze of towers and palaces and houses. And *think*!

[*Again he taps his forehead with a furious urgency.*]

Use your heads, eh? Use your flaming heads! There are fat men down there rich enough and vain enough to eat off gold plates. And stinking beggars crawling about in the dust for a tiny scrap of rubbish to keep them alive for one more miserable day. Is that right? Can that be right? There are men down there with *swords* ready to use for the sake of what they call their *glory*. Tcha! Is that right? Can that be right? Look at all the *pointless* suffering. The greed. Extortion. Exploitation. The killing. The pomp and swagger and hunger. Priests who talk about the love of God and hold out a collecting box at the same time. Soldiers trained to put a lance into the belly of another mother's son. Can all this be right? Eh? Why—a fool can see that it isn't!

[*Pause. A change of tone. The others are enraptured.*]

A fool. Yes. And perhaps *only* a fool, an idiot, can see what is so wrong with the world. Why else do people put up with it? Eh? *If* they knew the truth they would gather on the street corners in order to be sick. Now *that* would be a meaningful sacrament! Eh? But people don't know the truth. That's obvious. That's flaming obvious! They carry on with their jobs and their burdens and their burnt-out hopes. They don't stop in the middle of the street and shout, '*Why?*' And if they did they'd be put away. Look at me. Eh? I ought to be sawing wood or making benches and tables. Mmm? If I had any sense —*who is this coming*?

[*The question has a weird urgency—like a whipcrack of premonition. The others stare as* JUDAS ISCARIOT *approaches through the auditorium.*]

PETER [*aggressively*]: Hey—what do you want? Who are you?
JUDAS [*puffing*]: I have come out from Jerusalem—
JESUS: Jerusalem?
JUDAS: Yes. To—um—is there one here known as Jesus of Nazareth?

[*Slight pause.*]

Well?

JESUS: Is this Jesus known of in Jerusalem, then?

[JUDAS *stares at him, then smiles.*]

JUDAS: It is you. You are Jesus. But somehow you look—different. When you're not preaching.

JESUS: What do you want of me?

JUDAS: Peace of mind.

JESUS [*slight smile*]: Is that all?

[*The others laugh, still suspicious of a stranger.*]

JUDAS [*raised voice*]: The world is a wicked, wicked place!

[*Slight pause.*]

JESUS: God made it.

JUDAS: But—

JESUS: So perhaps we do not see all of it. Perhaps we who cannot grow one hair on our heads by an effort of will—well, perhaps we are not in a position to judge.

JUDAS: There is a good, and a bad.

JESUS: There is that!

JUDAS: Then how can I see the good and prepare myself for the Kingdom of Heaven?

[*Slight pause.*]

JESUS [*level toned*]: Honour the Commandments.

JUDAS: Pardon?

JESUS: Love God your Father above all things. And love your neighbour as yourself.

JUDAS: Who is my neighbour?

JESUS: The man next to you. Or him in the corner of your eye. [*dryly*] You can't miss him.

JUDAS: I try to follow the Commandments.

JESUS: Good.

JUDAS: What else must I do?

JESUS: Go home and sell all your possessions and give the money to the poor.

JUDAS: Or to the Temple?

JESUS [*bitingly*]: The poor!

JUDAS: And then?

JESUS: And then follow me. Give up everything else—family, friends, money, security—and come with me. We are about to—*illuminate* this land.

[JUDAS *suddenly sinks to his knees.*]

JUDAS: Yes, I will follow you.

[JESUS *smiles and touches* JUDAS' *head.*]

JESUS: What is your name?

JUDAS: Judas Iscariot.

JESUS: Welcome, Judas.

[*He embraces him.*]

JUDAS: My L—l—lord—?

JESUS: Yes?

JUDAS: Jerusalem is full of rumours about you. Some even dare to say that you are—

[*He stops.*]

JESUS [*quietly*]: I am that I am.

JUDAS: That you—you are the—Messiah.

[*Silence.*]

JESUS: Is that what they say?
JUDAS: *Are you?*

[*Silence.*]

JESUS: I am that I am.
JUDAS: But—Jesus—?
PETER: Leave him be!
JUDAS: Jesus—!

[JESUS, *strangely agitated, has gone to the cross. It is as though
he has just seen it, just realised what is there.*]

[*with urgency*] Jesus—Be *careful.* Please be careful.

[JESUS *throws back his head and roars with laughter.*]

JESUS: Careful! Have you trecked out all this way to tell me to be
careful!

[*The four others join in his laughter.*]

JUDAS [*shrilly*]: They'll nail you up on the Cross!

[*The laughter dies.*]

[*embarrassed*]: If you put a foot wrong—it's *that* horrible
thing . . .

[*He points at the cross. The others, except* JESUS, *automatically
cringe back from it.*]

ANDREW: I didn't even see it—I didn't even . . .
JESUS [*harshly*]: It is part of the landscape.

[*Silence.*]

JAMES [*agitated*]: Come on. I—suddenly I don't like this place.
ANDREW: Me neither. By God, no!

[*But* PETER, *who has been glaring at* JUDAS, *suddenly bursts out angrily at the newcomer.*]

PETER: What do you want? Eh? What do you have to say *that* for!
JUDAS: It is a warning.
PETER: Well stuff your bloody warning—
JESUS [*interrupting*]: Peter!
PETER: Well—he comes out here, all poshed up, and starts—
JESUS [*severely*]: *Peter!*

[JESUS *looks closely at* JUDAS, *who lowers his eyes.*]

[*quietly*] I understand where you are from. I understand what you are saying. But what is written is written. What is foretold is foretold.

[*The others are out of it; this is between* JESUS *and* JUDAS. *They listen, but only half-understand.*]

JUDAS: Then you are *He*?
JESUS: Perhaps. [*A little smile.*]
JUDAS [*imploring*]: Don't you *know*?
JESUS: God does not cheat.
JUDAS: I don't understand—?
JESUS: The son of man must be a man. He must be all of a man.
He must pass water like a man. He must get hungry and feel

tired and sick and lonely. He must laugh. He must cry. He cannot be other than a man, or else God has *cheated*.

JUDAS: But Jesus—if—

JESUS [*urgently*]: And so my Father in Heaven will abandon me to myself. And if my head aches he will not lift the ache out of it. And if my stomach rumbles he will not clean out my bowels. And if a snake curls into my thoughts, then the fang will be in my mind. If I were to have *no* doubt I would be *other than a man*.

[*Pause.*]

And God does not cheat.

[*Pause.*]

JUDAS: Then how shall we know?

JESUS: By what you see. By what you hear. How else?

[*Again* JUDAS *points at the cross.*]

JUDAS: Then you know—that thing! You know it waits for you.

JESUS [*very calm*]: It waits.

[*Silence. The others want to go.*]

JOHN: We don't like it here, Master.

PETER: *That* thing!

JAMES: Let us go down into the village—

ANDREW: Please. Jesus—

JOHN: We *don't like it* here!

[JESUS's *calm is shattered by their whimpering. His own fear bubbles to the top. He rounds on them, almost savagely.*]

JESUS [*with harsh mockery*]: 'We don't like it here, Master.' Too
  bad. Too flaming bad, my friends. Just look at that cross. Go
  on! Look at it!
PETER [*angrily*]: Why should we?
JESUS: So that we can keep it in our minds.

[*He taps angrily at his forehead.*]

Keep it in here. Keep the shape stinging behind our eyes. And
let one little splinter of that bloodied wood stick and fester in
our brains. Right?

[*He strides up to the cross and holds the upright beam, clinging to it.*]

God won't let me alone. Not now. I am His. Oh, oh. He
burns inside me. He tears at my chest. He lights up my eyes.
He tugs at my clothes. Oh Holy Father, you have hunted me
down. You have opened the top of my head. I have heard you.
I have seen you. Dear Lord God on High—shall I show a man
a chair, or shall I show man the truth of your justice and the
path to your Kingdom?

[*Feverish now, and impressive. The others kneel, except* JUDAS,
who stares wide-eyed at JESUS.]

Oh, oh, He burns inside me! The Lord God is in my head and
in my eyes and in my heart and in my mouth. Yes, in my
mouth. He has told me what to do, what to say. I am His. I
am His. I am His. I am the Chosen One. I am the Way.
I am the Messiah. Yes. Yes!

[*Pause.* JESUS *lowers his arms. Now he is calm and matter-of-fact.*]

Go into Jerusalem all of you, one by one. Tell the people

about Jesus of Nazareth. Tell them He is the One. The One they have been waiting for. Tell them that in three days I shall enter the Holy City on an ass, so fulfilling the prophesies of our forefathers. Tell them to greet me as they would their King. But it is the Kingdom of God I come to honour. Go now! Do as I say! Go! Go!

[*They rise and move off, and* JESUS *turns back to smack at the cross.*]

[*smiling*] Ach! You should have stayed a tree. A tree.

[*Slight pause.*]

And I should have stayed a carpenter. A carpenter.

[*Pause. Then he follows the others. The light fades.*]

SCENE 4

[PILATE'*s residence.* PILATE, *naked except for a towel, is being oiled by an attractive young servant girl. She is Jewish, and called* RUTH.]

PILATE [*grunting*]: Ah. Lovely. Lovely. Slap it on, girl. I want my muscles to loosen, and my skin to *gleam*. Mmm?
RUTH [*as in a dream*]: Yes, your Excellency.

[*Silence. She works away.* PILATE *is staring at her.*]

PILATE: You seem like one in a dream.

[*She smiles, almost to herself.*]

Rub it in. It is soo-thing. And won't do your hands any harm, either.

RUTH: No. Your Excellency.

PILATE: Expensive stuff!

[*No response.*]

[*irritated*] I said it is expensive oil!

RUTH: Yes. Your Excellency. As befits your Excellency.

PILATE [*mumbles*]: Very expensive oil . . .

[*Silence. She massages his chest. A sensual gleam in* PILATE'*s eyes.* RUTH *is—not too gladly—aware of it.*]

PILATE: You have very nice hands.

[*She does not reply.*]

I love women with long, cool fingers.

[*She does not reply.*]

[*rising tone*] D'you hear me, girl?

RUTH: Yes. Your Excellency. Would you like to turn so that I can oil your back, Your Excellency?

PILATE: Oh, all right.

[*He flops heavily over like a stranded whale. She works away.*]

What is your name, girl?

RUTH: Ruth. Your Excellency.

PILATE: Ruth?

RUTH: Yes. Your Excellency. It is a common enough name.

PILATE: Here, perhaps. In Judaea.

RUTH: Yes. Your Excellency.

PILATE: I like your hands, girl.

RUTH: Yes. Your Excellency.

PILATE: No, Your Excellency. Yes, Your Excellency. Have you no *life* in you? No *spirit*?

RUTH: I don't understand, Your Excellency.

PILATE: Tcha!

[*His flesh quivers with indignation.*]

RUTH: It is done now, Your Excellency.

PILATE: No. Put some more on. I want to *gleam*, you understand?

RUTH [*slight sigh*]: Yes. Your Excellency.

[*She pours oil on to his back straight from the jug. He jerks up, startling her.*]

PILATE: Great thundering heavens, what are you doing!

RUTH: I—I'm sorry, sir. You said you wanted a lot—

PILATE: Not to drown in the stuff, girl. Come here! Come!

[*She approaches him with lowered eyes. He slaps her viciously across the head.*]

I don't like carelessness!

RUTH: N-no Your Excellency.

PILATE: Slovenly people. All of you. Or downright subversive.

RUTH: Yes. Your Excellency.

[*He contemplates her. She hangs her head and twists her hands, looking very young.*]

PILATE: Did it hurt?

RUTH: No, Your Excellency.
PILATE: Proud, silly people! *Did it hurt?*

[*Pause.*]

RUTH: No, Your Excellency.
PILATE [*bellows*]: Then come here! Come on!

[*She again approaches. He knocks her to the ground.*]

Did *that* hurt? Did it?
RUTH: No!

[*She pulls herself up and goes over to him again.*]

You may hit me again. Your Excellency.
PILATE: What?

[PILATE *stares at* RUTH.]

RUTH: Hit me!
PILATE: You stupid girl. What are you trying to do? Are you *mad*?
RUTH [*blazing inside*]: No, Your Excellency. I cannot be mad. No!
PILATE [*frowning*]: Cannot?

[*She straightens proudly.*]

RUTH: I have seen the Messiah, praise God, and I am following
His way, His truth, and you cannot and you will not hurt me.

[*This delivered without bravado, and with total conviction. He
leaps at her and grabs her by the arms.*]

PILATE: *Who, girl? Who? Who?*

[*She answers with a sort of held-down gaiety.*]

RUTH: The Messiah. I have seen Him and *touched* Him.

[PILATE *lets go his grip, and stares at her, almost fearfully.*]

PILATE: What is his name? His name?
RUTH: His name is not to be told to the heathen.

[PILATE *again slaps at her.*]

He has come! He has come on an ass into our Holy City. He is now among us, and I am not afraid. I am not afraid.

[PILATE *again lifts his fist. And then, frowning, puzzled, lowers it.*]

You see, Your Excellency! What He has said is *true*. I—am—not—afraid.

[PILATE *turns away his head.*]

SCENE 5

[*The Temple in Jerusalem. Hubbub: a throng of people is spilling down into the auditorium. There are two tables for the money-changers.*]

MONEY CHANGER: Two of Tiberius, that is now the rate—two to the full ounce . . .

[*Lots of noise. Then—like dervishes—*PETER, JAMES, ANDREW *and* JOHN *burst in from all sides. Silence falls slowly—that of* *incredulity. The* FOUR DISCIPLES *clap their hands above their heads.*]

PETER [*clap—clap*]: *He* is coming!
ANDREW [*clap—clap*]: He is *here* among us!
JAMES: The Chosen One!
JOHN [*clap—clap*]: Make way. Listen! Listen all to Jesus of Nazareth.
PETER: Jesus of Nazareth!
ANDREW: Jesus of Nazareth!

[*The consternation is predictable. People gape at them.*]

PETER: He is coming! He is—here!

[*He points his huge arm and* JESUS *walks quietly forward out of the shadows and stands stock still. There follows a weird hush. An irritated* MONEY-CHANGER *breaks the spell.*]

MONEY-CHANGER: All right, all right. The rate is two of Tiberius against the full ounce . . .

[*He breaks off, startled, as an almost manic* JESUS *strides towards him.*]

JESUS: Shut up! Shut up!
MONEY-CHANGER: Now look here . . .
JESUS: You are in the House of Almighty God! Shut up, man! Does God care about your *rate*? Does He? Tcha!

[*He turns shouting, to harangue the gaping crowd. His voice is given added resonance by the colonnaded precincts.*]

Don't you know *where* you are, you people! Is the House of God no more than a squalid market place? Look at you! Look

at yourselves! Babbling and bargaining and burbling—
bringing your drudgeries and your greeds and your millstones
into the very cool, calm heart of your Maker! Aren't you
ashamed of yourselves? Do you think God is not aware of all
this? Do you think God does not see into your hearts and minds?

[*Silence.* JESUS *holds himself stiff and still, deliberately still.*]

Father?

[*Silence.*]

My Fa-ther?

[*Fractional pause.* JESUS *suddenly crumples, but still stands. He
claps his hands to the top of his skull, as though warding off hard
blows.*]

He—is—SPEAKING—to me. To me-ee-ee!

[*People pull back.* JESUS *is isolated. And he becomes 'possessed'.
Slowly, terribly slowly, he falls to his knees, hand gripping at his
throat, vibrating the words, mutating and strangling and yet
amplifying* them. *His legs thrash about.*]

Oh—Father—here—in—upon—at—*me*—here! You are—*Dada*
you are—near. NEAR. Nearnearnearnearnearnear—HERE!
Father! I am your—oh, oh—leave me! Leave me! [*sobs*] Yes!
What must I do-o-o-o?

[*Silence. He stops writhing. He is still, and composed, on his knees;
his arms limp at his sides, as though broken. Then he speaks again;
But now his voice is weirdly calm, flat, almost unhuman in its total,
mechanical lack of inflexion.*]

I see you I really see you at you see you at last all colour all dark all light all shade full empty now on the tide of the sea the curling of a leaf on the face of man all men on the pink spread of dawn soft the ooze of dream in the blackness of night and held between eyelids lace like and hair the wing of a bird stare of an eye kiss of lips kiss kiss of lips and in the even in the dung and the slime puss piss snail snake scab in the scream the torment the fever of the sick in the words in the silence the gap between the sigh the laugh the cry the gesture taking words from the air in love and again in love in love given in love unrequited in the thrust and fall and thigh and odour and the leap inside the leap to you which is you is you is you in all in every in there in here and here and now out of a mist shaped not shaped now. Here. Here. [*shouts*] Here!

[*Silence.*]

PETER [*shocked*]: He is here! Here Among Us.
ANDREW [*sobs*]: Je-sus. Je-sus.
OTHERS: Je-sus. Je-sus.

[*At the chanting of his name, which swells up also from the auditorium,* JESUS *appears to surface again, from a mystic trance. He stands, arms lifting, and yelling the chant.*]

JESUS: Peace! Peace! Peace!

[*Silence.*]

Yes! I AM HE!

[*Hubbub.*]

And this is My Father's house. It is here He spoke to me. He lets me speak to you. Listen then to me. I am the Way. I am the Light. The burden is mine and mine alone. This is my House.

[*He looks all around, accusingly.*]

Do you expect the Son of Man to sit down in dirt and talk through cobwebs? Do you expect to get near to God through the chink chink chink of *coin*? Do you expect to praise Him on a heap of silver? Listen to me. Clean up your minds. Think of the Lord God who is my Father in Heaven. Clear away the debris *behind* your eyes. Clear away the debris *in front* of your eyes! Clear it away! Away! You are here to praise Him.

[*Pause.*]

You are here to praise ME.

[*A long embarrassed pause.*]

MONEY-CHANGER [*rather nervously*]: All right—the rate to the ounce of sil—

[*He breaks off, astonished, as* JESUS, *totally without anger, strides over to him.*]

[*half-rising*] Wha—? What—?

[*But without breaking stride,* JESUS *upturns the* MONEY-CHANGER's *table. The coins scatter away.*]

[*angrily*] Look here you—!

[JESUS *raises an arm and points.*]

JESUS: *Go!*

[*Pause. With a sudden droop of the shoulders, the* MONEY-CHAN-GER *turns away.*]

PEOPLE: Je-sus! Je-sus! Je-sus!

[*Silence as* JESUS *turns, all authority now, and looks at the other* MONEY-CHANGER'*s table. But—and it must seem amazing—the* 2ND MONEY-CHANGER *stands and bows his head, in a tiny gesture of obedience: and overturns the table himself. A shocked pause.*]

JESUS: Are you with me?
2ND MONEY-CHANGER: Yes. I am with you. Always I have longed to do what I have just—

[JESUS *holds up his hand.*]

JESUS: All those here who are not with me are against me.
PETER [*shouts*]: We are with you!
ALL [*shout*]: We are with you!

[JESUS *smiles, but—almost imperceptibly—shakes his head.*]

JESUS: It is easy now to say you are with me. Words fly up like a bird startled in the nest. Will you who say you are with me still be with me another day, another week, another month from now?
1ST HECKLER: Give us a sign! A sign!
JESUS: What? What did you say?
1ST HECKLER: If you are from God then show us! Give us a sign, master!

[*His companions jeeringly take up the taunt.*]

HECKLERS: Go on! Give us a sign! Show us! Go on!

[*Some of the audience unwittingly, and eagerly, take up the cry.*]

VOICES: A sign—a sign . . .

[JESUS *holds up his arms for silence.*]

JESUS: A sign? [*gratingly*] What sort of sign?
IST HECKLER: If you are from God—I say, *if*—

[JESUS *pounces on him, his finger tracking him down.*]

JESUS: That man! Yes! You! Come closer! A sign. You want a sign?

[*Identified, and pushed forward, the* HECKLER *is not quite so confident*

IST HECKLER: If—If y-you are from God—

[JESUS *hurls his finger at him, eyes blazing.*]

JESUS: A thunderbolt! Will that do!

[*The people scurry away from the* HECKLER, *leaving him isolated and quaking.*]

IST HECKLER: I—I—only—
JESUS [*spitting*]: Temple policeman! I could crackle the flames through your limbs! Temple policeman!
IST HECKLER: No . . . no . . .
JESUS: Only a godless generation asks for a sign! You want to see the corn *before* it is planted! Oh, you hypocrite! I know you for what you are . . .

2ND HECKLER: Master, Master, shall we pay taxes to the Romans? Shall we acknowledge the rule of the *heathen*?
1ST HECKLER: Tell us what to do! Tell us!

[JESUS *stares at them. Then pulls in the crowd for support.*]

JESUS: You see! You see how they try to trap me!

[*Some mumbles of anger. Again, the* HECKLER *looks uncomfortable.*]

2ND HECKLER: It's—just that you can tell us what—
JESUS [*interrupting*]: Give me a coin!
2ND HECKLER [*confused*]: Wha?

JESUS: A coin. A coin. Give me a coin. [*to* OTHERS] It's all right. I'm not going into the collecting box business! Let us leave *that* to the priests!

[*Laughter.*]

Well—have you got one?
2ND HECKLER: Y-yes.
JESUS: Look at it.

[*The* HECKLER *gapes at it.*]

Whose head does it show? On the coin?
2ND HECKLER: Caesar's.
JESUS: Right. Then give to Caesar what belongs to Caesar. And give to God what belongs to God. *And shut up!*

[*Laughter.*]

Now, my friends, now I will tell you what belongs to God. *You* belong to God. You do not *belong* to Caesar. You belong to

God. What does that mean? It means that you belong to yourself. And it means that you belong to each other. You are all free. But you do not know that you are free. Come closer. Come. Come to me. I will tell you things kept secret since the world began. Do you *know* what it is to be a man? Come. Come and listen. Dare to listen. If I tell you how to change the world—and I *will* tell you how to change the world—oh, yes—well, then, they will try to silence me! What is written is written. What is foretold is foretold. But first you must listen. A light must be lit. The world need not always be in darkness. The world need not always be torn by soldiers and profiteers. The world need not always be filled with the hungry. Come. Come and listen. There are better things than have yet been seen. I will show you.

[*They all gather round him. The lights fade slowly. In the darkness the name of* JESUS *is murmured in a slowly growing crescendo of intensity and conviction.*]

SCENE 6

[PILATE's *residence. Night. A politico-military briefing is taking place between* PILATE, *the* COMMANDER *and a few other senior* ROMAN OFFICERS. PILATE *is pacing up and down in a furious agitation. The hawk-like* COMMANDER *stays erect, self-controlled, Roman.*]

PILATE [*flapping arms*]: Jesus! Jesus! *That's* who I want to know about! Understand?
COMMANDER: We have him cornered in the foothills, sir.
PILATE [*gapes*]: Jesus of Nazareth?
COMMANDER: Jesus Barabbas, sir.

PILATE: Barabbas? Cornered?

CAPTAIN: Holed up in a cave, sir.

CENTURION: We'll get him out, all right, sir.

PILATE: But the Nazarene—?

COMMANDER [*contemptuously*]: Oh, *that* Jesus. No problem, sir. No problem at all.

PILATE: Oh? Is that so?

CAPTAIN: Just a demented preacher, your Excellency. Of course we keep an eye on him . . .

PILATE: Fools! Damned fools!

COMMANDER: Beg your pardon, sir?

PILATE: Soldiers! The trouble with the military is that your brains are on the end of your swords!

COMMANDER [*annoyed*]: Sir?

PILATE: Jesus Barabbas is of *minor* importance—

CAPTAIN: He's led us a merry dance, sir.

CENTURION: A capable leader, sir . . .

PILATE: Yes, yes, yes. And we shall put him down as we shall put down all such stupid insurrections.

COMMANDER [*dryly*]: With our *swords*, sir. Not our words.

[*The insolence is too obvious. There is a dreadful pause.* PILATE *steps slowly to the* COMMANDER, *who remains erect and unblinking, and suddenly thrusts his face into the* COMMANDER's.]

PILATE [*hisses*]: You fool! You bloody, bloody fool!

COMMANDER [*barks*]: Sir!

[PILATE *keeps thrusting his face into the* COMMANDER's *face as he talks, with the sudden pecking and bobbing motion of a hen picking up seed.*]

PILATE: Your brains are in your lance. Your lance. It is not the force of arms we Romans have to worry about, sir!

COMMANDER [*barks*]: Sir!

PILATE [*hisses*]: But *ideas*, soldier. *Ideas*. [*insolently*] You know what an idea is? Mmm? Mmm? No? Well I'll tell you. An idea is stronger than an army, sharper than a lance, more enduring than an empire and more slippery than an eel. Ideas are what we fear. You understand? No—how could you? You've got Jesus Barabbas in some cave or other, like I knew you would. And we'll stretch him out, all right. But Jesus Nazareth—mmm? No soldiers, right? Love your enemies, right? A harmless idiot whom we might even use, right? He's not holed up in a cave with a cup of water and a gallon of bravado. He's holed up in the Temple—yes, the bloody Temple where we can't get at him. Though if I had my way . . . Anyway the people have suddenly, all at once, like—like—a flash of lightning— they've decided he really *is* the Messiah.

COMMANDER [*sarcastic*]: Really, sir? Another one?

PILATE: Dunderhead! Thick, thick idiot!

COMMANDER [*blinking*]: Sir?

PILATE: This is the one they've been waiting for. Even my own servants believe in him. I had a girl flogged to death and still the little fool would not deny him. He is inside us, like a ravening wolf. He is the spark that can set this whole province alight. Once the Jews believe he *is* their leader we have a load of trouble on our hands. And cunning old Caiaphas will be helpless, too.

CAPTAIN: Can't we go in there and drag him out, sir? That'll soon put a stop to it.

[PILATE *claps his hands to his head in mock despair.*]

PILATE: Oh save me from the military mind!

CAPTAIN [*abashed*]: Sorry, sir.

[*Inexplicably,* PILATE *becomes suddenly affable. Perhaps it is because he wants to show how superior his own mind is, and enjoys the demonstration.*]

PILATE: You see, if *we* grab him, inside or outside the Temple, we shall only confirm his status in the eyes of the people. We shall have total riot on our hands. No. The thing to do is to rope in that wily old bird, Caiaphas. See? Now he doesn't want a religious fanatic on his hands, does he? What Priest ever wanted his religion to be taken *too* seriously?

[*The others laugh dutifully, except the still smarting* COMMANDER. PILATE *pokes him playfully in the ribs.*]

Oh come on, misery bones!

[*A leathery little smile satisfies* PILATE.]

So—*so* we let the Jews deal with their own damned Messiah. And we make *sure* that they do by turning the screw on their own authorities. All those in power understand power. We talk the same language. Caiaphas has kept his people together by demanding this, conceding that. We have kept overall authority by conceding this, demanding that. It is the language of politics, the dialogue of common sense. We threaten to replace Caiaphas. We threaten to plunder the Temple coffers. Oh, a host of things! Then they will understand. And deal with this—this fanatic. And once this Jesus has been properly *and fairly* tried by the Jewish Court he will be by law handed over to the Civil Power. To me. And there's an end of it!

SCENE 7

[The Temple. Night. CAIAPHAS *and* JUDAS *are walking up and down together.]*

CAIAPHAS: Come, Judas, Come! I have seen and heard him myself! He abuses the priesthood mercilessly.

JUDAS *[distressed]*: But—but—Master, the things he talks about *have* happened—with respect, Master, there are . . .

CAIAPHAS *[interrupting]*: Bad and hypocritical priests. Agreed, agreed. We live in filthy and corrupt times.

JUDAS: And he has come to cleanse!

CAIAPHAS: You are *sure*?

JUDAS: I am sure. Now I am sure.

CAIAPHAS: I would like to think so, too. His dream is—my dream. He has therefore nothing to fear from the Temple Court. Has he? Mmm? The people are saying he *must* be the Messiah because we do not interfere with him. Isn't that so?

JUDAS: Yes. But—

CAIAPHAS: You love him, Judas?

JUDAS: Yes!

CAIAPHAS: Then save him from himself. His rhetoric is getting out of hand. Why—he compares the priests with whitened sepulchres! And the surest way to destroy a faith is to destroy the standing of its earthly representatives. Surely you must see that!

JUDAS *[hesitantly]*: Yes, Master—

CAIAPHAS: And surely the properly sanctified priesthood has not only the right but the *duty* to inspect his claims and make some sort of pronouncement upon them and so upon him for the guidance of our flock?

JUDAS: But why should he be arrested? Master! Please! It degrades him—and if—it—it—

CAIAPHAS: Judas, Judas. Do you trust me?

[*Pause.* CAIAPHAS *tightens his grip on* JUDAS' *shoulder.*]

JUDAS: Yes, Master.

CAIAPHAS: You don't sound too sure!

JUDAS [*ashamed*]: Oh, Master!

CAIAPHAS: You see—he is sowing dissent and distrust. Until his claim can be properly examined we shall all be in danger. Now, why has he fled the Temple?

JUDAS: He—well, it seemed prudent . . .

CAIAPHAS [*bitingly*]: Is a Messiah *prudent*?

[*Silence.*]

JUDAS: And—and—he wanted to m-m-meditate . . .

CAIAPHAS: Tcha!

JUDAS [*angrily*]: All right! All right, then! He will *prove* he is from God before you and all the Priests—

CAIAPHAS: Judas. That is all I want! And—oh—*how* I want it!

[*Silence.*]

JUDAS: I—I must of course do as you ask. I will take the police to him. I—I—

[JUDAS *cannot speak.*]

CAIAPHAS [*gently*]: You are doing what is right. And, if he is what he says he is, he has nothing, *nothing* to fear from me or *any* man!

[JUDAS *goes out.*]

[*Kneeling*] Almighty God, have you sent us the One, at last? . . . Almighty God . . . ?

86

SCENE 8

[*Gethsemane. Night.* PETER *and* ANDREW *are asleep, coiled into each other.* JESUS *is on his knees, a little way apart. We hear the sound of wind.*]

JESUS: Father! Father! Is it *me*? Is it? Is it? Is it *me*? *Me!*

[*He collapses, sobbing, to lie flat on the ground. The sobs slowly subside, and wearily he pulls himself up.*]

[*between his teeth*] They will nail me up. It is written so. If I am *He—*

[*He thumps at his chest: then cries out loud.*]

Oh God! God! You are *burning* inside me! *Burning!* So why am I fearful? *Why?*

[*He walks over to* PETER *and* ANDREW *and looks down at them sleeping. He smiles.*]

Oh, fishers of men . . . [*loudly*] Peter!

[PETER *stirs, smacking his lips.*]

PETER: Wha? Wha? Master?
JESUS: Where are the others?

[PETER *gapes around him.*]

PETER: They—um—we all—um—I don't know—

[*He scratches his head.*]

JESUS [*hisses*]: Pray for me! Pray for me!

SCENE 9

[*The Temple. In a pool of light we see* CAIAPHAS, *alone, at prayer. There is a moment's intense silence. Then* CAIAPHAS *lifts his head, tears rolling down his face, and whispers.*]

CAIAPHAS: He can still save himself. Still.

[*He stays.*]

SCENE 10

[*Gethsemane. Night.* JESUS, PETER, ANDREW *are huddled together.* JUDAS *and others approach through the auditorium.*]

PETER: Look! The torches! They have come for us like you said!
ANDREW: Let's run—run—

[JESUS *catches at him.*]

JESUS: No Andrew. No. What must be, must be. It is what I must —*accomplish.*
PETER: It's because you mocked the Priests—
JESUS [*gaily*]: Yes! Yes, I did!

[JAMES *and* JOHN *rush on, frightened. A crowd is approaching, with burning torches, sticks, cudgels, swords.*]

JUDAS [*agitated*]: Stay back! Stay back! I *told* you. No violence—it is not n-necessary—stay back I say!

[*He walks forward, head bowed. The others hang back.*]

JESUS [*unsure*]: Judas?
JUDAS: Yes, Master.
JESUS: *You!*
JUDAS: Yes, Master. You must prove yourself before the Temple
    Court.

[JESUS *laughs harshly*.]

PETER: You bastard!
JESUS: No, Peter. No.
JUDAS: I—I—Jesus. Are you the Messiah? *Are you?*

[JESUS *laughs, so gently*. JUDAS, *overcome, embraces him and kisses him on the cheek*.]

[*full of emotion*] Oh, Jesus. Dear Jesus. Please come with us.
    Please. There is no other way.
JESUS [*whispers*]: No—no other way.

[JUDAS *puts his head in his hands*.]

Don't worry about it. Don't worry Judas. Don't. Oh, don't.

SCENE II

[*The Temple. The end of the trial of* JESUS. CAIAPHAS, *fully robed, turns, and speaks with slow, massive solemnity*.]

CAIAPHAS: Have you nothing to say?

[*Pause*.]

Jesus of Nazareth, witness after witness has testified to your blasphemies. Blasphemies spoken here within the very walls of God's own dwelling. Yet you have not challenged them. You have not replied. You have not produced any witness to say differently.

[*Pause.*]

Jesus of Nazareth! Do you believe yourself to be inspired by Almighty God?

[*Pause.*]

Have you *nothing* to say?

[*Silence.*]

JESUS [*under stress*]: Nothing.

[JUDAS *shouts an impassioned plea from the sidelines.*]

JUDAS: Jesus! Answer them!
CAIAPHAS: Silence! Silence! This is an examination. Not a public debate. This is the Temple. Not babel.

[*Silence.* CAIAPHAS *begins to walk slowly towards* JESUS, *who is smiling slightly.* CAIAPHAS *stops.*]

You come wild and ragged and stinking out of the hills to throw abuse at the priests, elders and guardians of Almighty God.

[*Pause.* CAIAPHAS *steps one pace nearer, almost imploringly.*]

[*quietly*] Are you the Son of the Blessed One?

[*No answer.*]

[*louder*] Are you the Messiah?

[*No answer.*]

If you are, then *speak*. If you are not, you are the greatest blasphemer and hypocrite that ever walked God's earth. Speak! Speak! [*hisses*] Are you He? Son of the Blessed One? *Are—you—the—Messiah?*

[JESUS *stares back at him, seems about to answer, then drops his head.* CAIAPHAS *tears at* JESUS' *robes in a fury.*]

Blasphemer! Blasphemer! Need we go on! [*turns to* PRIESTS] This man, this Jesus, is obviously guilty. What say you? What say you?

[*Fractional pause, then big 'Aye' from chorus of* PRIESTS.]

PRIESTS: Aye!
JUDAS [*calling*]: Jesus! Jesus! Please! Please!
CAIAPHAS: Take that man out! Out!

[*Temple* GUARDS *drag out a protesting* JUDAS. *The hubbub dies.* CAIAPHAS *raises his arms for silence.*]

We are finished. We find Jesus of Nazareth guilty of heresy and the most foul of blasphemies against the Law and the Prophets.

[JESUS *laughs out loud.*]

He shall be bound in chains and delivered up to the Prefect of

Judaea for sentence. And let him be yet more warning to the confused, the gullible and the dissenting that here, in the Temple, only in the Temple, can one find the true, ordained authority of the Law of the Prophets. For this is the Seat of Moses, in the Holy City of God.

[*Pause.*]

Bind him! Take him away! Take him away!

[*About a dozen men leap on* JESUS, *binding his hands, blind-folding him, chaining him. He submits passively.* CAIAPHAS *watches for a moment with pursed lips, then turns away with a sweep of his robe.*]

SCENE 12

[PILATE's *Jerusalem residence. Bright lights and military bustle. The throng bring forward* JESUS, *chained and blindfolded.* PILATE *waits. He holds a scroll. He looks up, mild in manner and tone.*]

PILATE: Why did you give no answer to all these charges?

[*No reply.*]

These religious quarrels mean little or nothing to me, man. But I *have* to act upon this verdict unless I see good reason not to. You have said nothing in your own defence. Why?

JESUS: I have nothing to say.

[*Pause.*]

PILATE: You expect your God to say or do it for you. Is that right? Speak up, fellow.

PETER [*shouts*]: You cannot harm him!

ANDREW: God will take him from you!

[*Others take up the shouts. But the* SOLDIERS *move—menacingly. Silence.*]

PILATE: Are you the Messiah?

[*Slight pause.*]

JESUS: The word has no meaning for you. Yet.

PILATE: Are you the king of the Jews?

JESUS: Are those your words?

PILATE: To claim or even not to deny that you are the king of the Jews is to challenge the authority of the Emperor. It would be to countenance insurrection and to defy the religious autonomy of your own courts were I wantonly to set aside sentence. Can you say nothing in your own defence?

[*No reply.* PILATE *approaches* JESUS.]

Take off the blindfolds.

[*This is done.* PILATE *steps forward, thrusting his face at* JESUS, *staring at him with an ultimately rather comical intensity.*]

JESUS [*amused*]: Good afternoon.

[PILATE *stares. And then smiles with delight.*]

PILATE: Good afternoon. I'm rather afraid, though, that it will be your last.

JESUS: Perhaps.
PILATE: You must have known this would happen. You must have realised you were making too many enemies. You should have stayed out in the hills.

[JESUS *sort of shrugs.*]

Are you the Messiah? Is that what you claim to be?

[JESUS *laughs.*]

I have to pass sentence you know! The only sentence permitted is that of crucifixion. Aren't you afraid of the nails?

[*Pause.* PILATE *stares at him.*]

JESUS: Yes.
PILATE [*amused*]: Do you *love* your enemies?
JESUS: Yes.
PILATE: What about me? [*Mocking.*] Do you love me?

[*Pause.* JESUS *looks at him steadily.* PILATE'*s chuckle dies away uncomfortably.*]

JESUS: Yes, Pontius.

[PILATE *slaps out at him in humiliation. And then suddenly covers his face in a gesture of shame.*]

PILATE: I'm sorry. That was not necessary. That was not necessary.
JESUS: Don't be afraid.

[*This really frightens* PILATE.]

PILATE: *What?*
JESUS: There is no need to be frightened.

[PILATE *steps back in alarm. He shouts out in bewildered anger.*]

PILATE: Take him away! Take the idiot away! I confirm sentence.
He's had every chance. Every chance.
SHOUTS: Crucify him! Deliver us!

[*A disciplined squad of Romans march forward, deploy, and pull*
JESUS *away.* PILATE *watches. Then, with a bewildered, almost*
tormented gesture, turns away. The spotlight shines on JESUS *and*
the SOLDIERS, *down stage. The rest is darkness. Here the biblical*
account follows in all its brutality. JESUS *is systematically laid into;*
his clothes are torn, he is laughed and jeered at. SOLDIERS *circle*
round him, using his chains to whirl him round, pushing him from
one to the other in a vicious game. Then they whip him, savagely.]

FIRST SOLDIER: Here! Let's give him a crown! King of the Jews!
SECOND SOLDIER: Thorns—a crown of thorns . . .
JESUS [*croaks*]: No . . . no . . .

[*They beat him to the ground with horrible persistence. He is*
dragged, moaning, back on to his feet, spitting blood. They salaam
in front of him, roaring with laughter.]

SOLDIERS: Hail! King of the Jews! Hail! King of the Jews!

[*One of them kicks him in the groin to knock him down again. He*
is whimpering with pain. They pull him up, and whip him again.]

SCENE 13

[*Golgotha. The crucifixion.* JESUS *is hammered onto the cross. He screams in terrible agony as his hands are driven into the wood. As he is raised up he twists his head from side to side, moaning with agony. Then there is calm.*]

JESUS: Is it *me–e*?

[*Silence. He twists, twists.*]

It is me. It is me it is me it is me it is me . . .

[*His voice dies into a choke. Silence. Then he suddenly screams.*]

Father! Father! Why have you forsaken me . . .

[*A spurt of blood chokes the cry in his mouth. The lights fade, leaving a spotlight on the cross. Calm.* JESUS *is still, finished. Then he lifts his head in sudden triumph.*]

It—is—ACCOMPLISHED.

[*His head drops. It is all over. The spot slowly fades. Darkness. No sound.*]